The Christian Teen
DEVOTIONAL

RYAN RENCH

Calvary Baptist Publications
Calvary Baptist Church | Pastor W. M. Rench
31087 Nicolas Rd. Temecula, CA 92591
(951) 676-8700 | CalvaryBaptist.pub

Contents

READ FIRST: About This Devotional

JOURNAL

APPENDIX

READ FIRST:
About This Devotional

Introduction

I hate most devotionals.

I shouldn't say *hate*. Sorry.

Most devotionals stink.

I had one in high school that was called *What Planet Are My Parents From?!* Starting with the title, this devotional was terrible. It tried to make parents look like idiots while it was cool and relevant to teens.

Even as a teenager, I thought it was simple. And silly.

It had no depth, and the daily reading was minimal. The challenges were okay, but I was never sure if what THEY said actually lined up with what GOD said in His Word.

So I ditched it and just read my Bible straight through. I still prefer that method.

You Need Your OWN Reading Plan

This devotional is like a dietary supplement... it's taken **in**

addition to your meal.

This devotional does NOT have a reading schedule, does not discuss specific passages of Scripture, and does not have a set schedule to follow.

I hope you have a schedule set up already. Here are a few ideas:

- **3-4 Chapters Daily.** For my teens to qualify for missions trips, I have them read 3-4 chapters per day, which takes them through the Bible in a year. The first time I completed my Bible all the way through, this was the method I used.

- **Proverbs/Psalms.** Each chapter of Proverbs can correspond to the day of the month (i.e. read Proverbs 10 on January 10). Or, you can read 5 Psalms per day to cover the book (150 Psalms) in a month. This is a good starting point for people who are new to the habit of Bible reading.

- **New Testament—One Chapter**. If long reading seems daunting at first, start smaller. Go through a book one chapter at a time. Start with the Gospels (Matthew, Mark, Luke, John). You can't go wrong when you read about Jesus every day.

- **One Verse**. I know a pastor who, when he first became a Christian, started reading one verse per day. For a month. Then, the second month, he read exactly *two* verses per day. The third month, three. I'm ALL about starting small and building over *time*.

Then... What Is THIS Devotional?

This devotional is a series of notes that I wrote to my teens over the period of 7 years as their youth pastor. Every Sunday and Wednesday class, they receive an Announcement Sheet with words to the songs, details about activities and a short note.

I sorted the notes by category and arranged them into this book. Sometimes the notes are encouraging. Sometimes challenging. Sometimes humorous, silly, or for reference only.

But always—always—helpful in *some* way.

We try to put excellent content into teens' hands. When I was a teen, it was relieving to know that I could always find answers in good content. As a youth pastor, I want everything I put into my teens' hands to push them forward in their walk with the Lord.

And that's what this book is about—helping you grow closer to God.

Who Is It For?

Originally, these notes were for my teens, so you will read some notes that are specific to our church. However, the content goes beyond Calvary Baptist Church in Temecula, CA, and spreads to you, too.

If you are a **teen**, imagine it coming from the voice of your youth pastor—encouraging you to draw closer to God.

If you are a **youth pastor** or **parent**, you can use this book in a variety of ways:

- **Articulate.** If you are looking for new ways to communicate truth to young people, use this book as a reference for how to word something. For example: "How do I communicate *loving God*? Or how can I encourage my teens to care about missions?"

- **Think.** This book can spawn ideas for how you can communicate truths in new ways to your teens. If you use none of these words directly, you can use the seed ideas to emphasize certain topics in a new light.

- **Copy.** Sometimes you do not have the time to create the content directly yourself, so feel free to copy and distribute these. As long as it is attributed (and you're not pretending they are your words), I see no problem with passing out an article that might help people.

- **Disciple/Gift.** A book like this is great for gifting or using as an encouragement to teens. The notes are short enough to read in 5-minute increments, and pointed enough to teach good lessons over time.

How Should I Read It?

You can read this book several ways. Here are a few ideas:

- **Daily.** Set aside time each day to pray, read your Bible, and read one entry. I do NOT recommend this as your *only* devotional content, but as an **addition to** what you are already doing.
- **Straight Through.** Maybe you like binge-watching Netflix, so you want to binge-read a book like this, too. Go ahead! Read it straight through like you would any other book.
- **Topically.** Each section of the book covers a new topic. Sometimes there are 30 or more articles. Sometimes there are two. You might scan the Contents page to find a topic you are curious about.

I'm In!

You say, "I'm in! Let's get going."

Good. Let's do this.

I hope it's a help.

Loving God

If a teen can learn to love God with all his heart, he is set for life.

Anyone who truly has a love for God will do alright with the rest of the Bible. It is not a list of rules when you love God.

I loved and respected my dad growing up. I loved and respected my pastors in college. I wanted to please the influential men in my life because I loved them. I served them not out of fear, but out of a desire to help them in any way that I could.

Loving your heavenly Father takes care of a lot of problems in life. That is why I always say *love God, love others, and do right*.

You Need a Personal Relationship With God

I hope you grew in the Lord somehow this week. If you are a Christian, God WANTS to have a great relationship with you! Did you talk to him this week? Did you let him talk to you through his Word this week?

Many of you have made great decisions to do more and be more for God. God has gifted every one of you with some *incredible* tools, and he will absolutely bless your life if you use those gifts to edify others while at church. Did you encourage anyone last week? Did you write any notes, say "Amen!" in church, or shake Pastor's hand and tell him he's a blessing to you? You ought to! It will help YOU to be an encouragement to someone else!

How about helping? Did you offer to help out around the church? Did you attend the soul winning time in Redlands yesterday? (Praise God for the 13 that did!)

Every week, LOTS of opportunities surround you, and it will only help YOU if you follow God's leading in your life! Give yourself to him, and you'll never regret a minute of it! If He leads you to clean off your iPod, clean up your mouth, or be more faithful to church, it's not because he hates you and wants you to suffer... God LOVES you and wants what's best for you! I hope you realize that. I want to communicate that same love to you and others. If you EVER need anything, let us know!

God Didn't Do Anything Good This Week

"What?! Bro. Ryan, don't say that!" you might think.

You might be shocked at hearing that said... but have you LIVED this week like that's not true?

Did you thank Him today for something good He's done? You should have.

Did you think on His goodness today? You should have.

Did you even have a desire to spread that to someone at school today? You should have.

We're SO good at being SHOCKED when someone says something "unspiritual" like that, especially when it's coming from "the preacher." But are you that shocked when YOU'RE not thankful for the good things God's done?

You wicked Pharisee.

That's what they did! They were self-deceived. They saw lots of problems with everyone else and didn't think twice when it was THEIR OWN sin.

You might be able to know how to dress for church, what to say, and how to be respectful to your parents... tooty toot toot to you. How's your so-called commitment to purity? Are you staying as FAAAAAR away from "that gray area" as possible?

Or do you push it whenever you can?

How's your passion for Bible preaching? Did you increase the fervor of the Bible preaching ministry of our church last Sunday? If not, by definition you DEcreased the fervor.

"We go to a Bible preaching church." Tooty toot toot. What did YOU do to contribute?

We could go on and on. I'm very excited about the message tonight! Every time I preach I envision God's Word getting a hold of your hearts, and I envision RADICAL CHANGE. Every time I preach. I mean that. I'm rarely discouraged; I'm always waiting... anticipating.

I can't wait to see what God does with some of you wicked Pharisees. God has already torn me up over this text. I hope it's a help tonight.

Memorizing John 15 Should Help You Abide In God

John 15 is amazing. Abiding in the vine is the only way to bear fruit. Or... like the song says... "There's a grape on the leaf, and the leaf on the branch, and the branch on the vine, and the vine on the root, and the root in the hole, and the hole in the ground..." God's the vine (the trunk). We're the branches. We can't bear fruit without being connected to Him.

How? Through His Word. That's what the text says. I'm not twisting this and making it fit into our Bible Study series! It's just that pretty much everything about the spiritual life boils down to... the Bible!

Love it and live it.

Summer Break Doesn't Mean Spiritual Break

This note came at the end of the school year...

Summer. Don't you love that word?

Summer break. No school.

Don't take a break from church! In fact, the summer is always an awesome time for the TOF because we get to hang out that much more. You won't hear "It's a school night" for a few more months. ☺

I hope you dedicate your summer to God today. Determine now to grow in the Lord and serve Him better this break. Don't miss church. Don't miss youth activities. Come to everything. Be involved. Be a blessing.

Take a step back and look at your new "position" in the youth group. The seniors are leaving. Everyone's a year older. We'll be getting a few new members in our class as the 6th graders graduate in. You who are the youngest now... not for long! And that means everyone reading this will have a new job... you'll either create a good example or a bad one. Good examples are the ones who are a blessing, the ones who are welcoming, and the ones who take others under their wing and help them. Teach them the "unwritten rules." Help them understand some things. LOVE them!

Bad examples are the opposite. They don't care about anyone but themselves. They set a bad tone. They don't care about influencing everyone, and they think that by keeping to themselves they're fine... wrong! No one is neutral... you're either a good influence or a bad one. A bad influence might mean that you're a reprobate... but that's probably not you. More likely, you'll be a bad influence simply by not choosing to be a blessing. By just sitting there and not caring about anyone else, you're a bad influence.

I emphasize over and over... love God, love others, do right. "Well, I love God, but I just hate annoying people!" God calls you a liar! If you hate anyone, according to 1 John 4, you're a liar! That's not MY words... that's God's! So love everyone.

Love God. Love others. Do right. I sure love you!

New School Year. Fresh Start.

This note was for students starting a new school year...

I always view the new school year as a fresh start.

Like hitting the reset button on your life.

New classes. New teachers. New schedules. Sometimes even new schools.

Well, along with the new school year, youth groups also get a refresh. We're starting your school year off slow on purpose. There aren't many activities in the fall as you readjust to your new school calendars, and we kind of ease into your busy winter and spring with all the trips we'll be taking.

Hopefully you're beginning to think of this year as a year to make some really big spiritual changes in your life. That is MY prayer! I have prayed that God will use this year as a really special time, and that some of you will absolutely blossom in the Lord. I'm praying that some of you will be more bold than ever in your schools, that you'll reach more of your friends than ever before, that you'll see people saved, and that you'll be more fired up about the Lord and spiritual things than ever before.

What's it going to take? You have everything you need to live a fulfilled, abundant Christian life. Choose to live it this year! I love you and will be praying for you. Love God. Love others. Do right.

Love God. Love Others. Do Right.

Love God, teens. Love God more than anything else in life. When you do, your love for others grows and your desire to do right increases. Doing right shows. It changes your countenance. It means you forgive. It means you treat others like 1 Cor. 13 says you should. It means you have a renewed passion for God's Word. It means you watch what you say — gossip, bad language, "idle" speaking as the Bible says it... all these are gone (or you at least are working on it!) It means a lot of things. Love God. Love others. Do right. It's for your good.

Poop — Sacrifice It For the Best Things

This note came after a 4-day revival service...

What a blessing to see many of you here every night of our Revival. Your faithfulness during the school week is almost as valuable as the preaching itself!

When you get a real passion for the Bible you can't help but be revived. That's what the Bible does for you... it makes you MORE alive. That's how it can always be fresh even though it is so old. That is why it has been studied by every true Christian throughout the centuries and has never been exhausted.

The Bible is amazing, and I love to see you catching a glimpse of God through His Word.

I hope you spend time applying the Bible to your lives. It only takes maybe 10 or 20 minutes a day. Honestly, that's not a lot.

"Well, that takes too long, Bro. Ryan." Really? Really?

I think if you can be online and get your homework done and play Angry Birds and watch TV and sleep for 8 hours and... I think there's SOME time in there to be in your Bible. Maybe it will mean sacrificing some... poop (remember Wednesday night's sermon? Your iPod, your computer, your time, your friends...). In God's eyes it is all dung and only what you do for Christ will last.

Give up sleep for Christ? No problem.

What Does "Living For God" Mean?

This note was from the Sunday following a church member's funeral...

We use the term *Living for God* all the time.

Have you ever stopped and thought about that?

Do you live for God? You won't have another chance later on. You will never be able to relive your past. Someday when you're old and looking back... you'll never be able to live your teen years again. How much time are you wasting in bitterness? In selfishness? In resentment? In hate? In boring, lifeless, self-indulgence?

Do you live for God by living for others? Are you investing your life in things that will matter? Or are you wasting your time.

Mrs. Anasarias passed away on Friday night, but she was a lady who lived for God. Her life was about serving God and others, and right up to the end, her testimony was that she lived for God. My wife, Pastor and I were able to be with the final moments with the family, and her hospital room was filled with coworkers and family. Everyone nodded in agreement when Pastor made the statement that she lived for God.

Whether you know it or not, people will know you by how you live. Sometimes you reflect a little deeper on your own life when it is threatened, or when a precious loved one is lost. Think about your life... how will you be remembered? As someone who was faithful? As someone who lived for God?

We are grieving with the Anasarias family in their loss. No doubt. But it was amazing to see that in the middle of all that grief, the family was able to be a beacon of hope to everyone in the room by affirming their confidence in Mrs. Eileen's home in heaven. There was no doubt. There was no hoping. They didn't have to light a candle or pray really hard that she would go to heaven. They knew without doubt that they will see mom again. It is difficult, confusing and painful to lose a loved one, but God's light is brightest when it's the darkest time of night.

Do You Love God? Or Not?

Do you love God?

Of course, Bro. Ryan. He saved me.

Sure. Everyone says they love God. But do you really love God? I'm not talking about being thankful for your salvation. I'm talking about a life-changing, no-faking it kind of love. THAT kind of love should drive everything you do as a Christian.

You have probably heard me say more than once that the Christian life is not a list of do's and don'ts. It's not a checklist you follow. It's not a drudgery.

When you have a true relationship with God, everything else takes care of itself. Sure, we have certain rules and dress codes and things for church activities or camps, but we wouldn't necessarily need a rulebook if everyone loved God as deeply as they should.

Loving God is self-sacrificial. Have you sacrificed anything lately? Loving God means you don't want to hurt others. What did you post this week? Loving God means you hate sin and love righteousness. Love covers basically everything. When you passionately love God, you're not forced to read your Bible because you have to. It's a joy! When your love for God is in the right place, you don't do your BIBS just so you can go on the Alaska trip, you do them because you want to understand and apply God's Word to your life! Loving God means that you recognize and repent of your own passive-aggressiveness and rather try to edify others with your words. Loving God means that you simply have a spirit that says, "Whatever God says to do, I'll do it with all my heart." No excuses. No lying. No faking it. True, real love.

Love God. Love others. Do right.

Don't Suffer From the Illusion of Spirituality

I've often said I'm not impressed with people who are all talk.

I'm not impressed until I see all your spiritual talk in action. You shouldn't be impressed either.

A lot of people who grew up in a Christian home and have a

good family automatically assume they're spiritual. You know all the right answers. Your mom and dad say the right things, so you parrot the right things as if they're your own.

When they really DO become your own is when you become spiritual. Until then, it's all just talk.

Anyone can say, "Yeah, I love others."

- But then why are you a snob?
- Or why do you laugh at others when they're just trying to fit in?
- Or why do you make fun of someone else's looks or the things they like?
- Or why do you avoid someone because you think he's dorky?
- Or why do you sneer at someone's comment as if you're better than him or her?
- Or why do you talk about others behind their back?
- Or why don't you work harder to welcome others?

You have the illusion of love, but it's not real.

Anyone can say, "I'm a servant."

- But can you be found when it's time to clean up?
- Are you the last one working, or do you stand around and talk and wait to be told what to do?
- Do you look for ways to serve or do you look for ways to get OUT of serving?
- Do you take initiative or find excuses?

You might have the illusion of being a servant, but if you don't serve... you're fake.

Anyone can say, "My parents are hypocrites."

How about you? You can't change others, but you can change you. Do YOU have the inward life that you're claiming on the outside?

Your BIBS section through James talked about this very thing. You can say, "be ye warmed and filled" but if "ye give them not those things which are needful to the body, what doth it profit?" What good are you if you're all talk? (James 2:14-16.) Your spirituality is just an illusion.

Don't just be a Christian on the outside. And don't just be a Christian on the inside. Be both.

I know how easy it is to slip back into knowing all the answers but not being able to connect it to real life.

Real life is, like,

- Loving others on Promotion Sunday
- Learning to live with and even love people you find annoying
- Loving people you used to hate
- Greeting guests
- Sitting next to lonely people
- Greeting adults at hand-shaking time
- Inviting people in our class to the campout
- Coming to door-knocking
- Cleaning up after pie fellowship

Basic day-to-day stuff.

Don't just allow the illusion of spirituality to blind you to who you really are. Daniel saw himself for who he really was and he was humbled. Isaiah saw himself compared to God and there was no illusion of spirituality there... he fell on his face humbled. Paul seemed like a spiritual man, but HE never considered himself a great guy.

Be truly spiritual, and let it show in a humble, obedient attitude.

Do You Love God?

I mean, REALLY love God? I'm not asking if you're saved. You might be saved and not love God.

The term itself is somewhat vague. "Love God." Ok. Sure. I love God... Love, love, love. Ok, am I done loving God now? What did I just do?

When I say, "Love God," usually it's just a broad generalization. It's usually an overarching concept that touches every part of your life.

"Loving God" is the best and easiest way for me to say that you should have a relationship with God. If you love God the way you should and truly remember what he has done for you, obeying Him is easy. You're compelled to obey. You're not forced to obey... you WANT to!

If you're in love with God, you won't have to be rewarded to read your Bible. You do it because you want to hear from God. With that mindset, it should take A LOT to make you miss your devotions. I mean, NO excuses. I mean, it HURTS you to miss a day. Not because you won't get the points on the sheet but because you missed your quiet time with your Father. Having a friend over shouldn't change anything about your devotions the next morning. Going to bed late because of finals homework shouldn't change your passion to have time with God.

If it's real, nothing gets in the way. Same with church. Nothing gets in the way of a true conviction about being in church. Same with a kind spirit, love, joy, peace, longsuffering, obeying your parents, being encouraging, welcoming others in class, serving, working hard, praying... you get the idea. EVERYTHING is affected by your love for God.

When GOD is the one convicting you of sin, helping you grow, pointing out your pride, showing you your weaknesses and using the Holy Spirit to help you grow, it doesn't have to be me, your parents, the Bakers or others pointing out areas you should improve on spiritually. When you're Christ-motivated instead of pleasing-authority-motivated, it changes everything. Maybe it doesn't change what you're doing, but it changes your heart behind it all. Don't merely do right. Love God and others truly. Then do right.

I'm 22 Years Old!

Yesterday was my *spiritual* birthday. When's yours?

By spiritual birthday I mean the day I got saved. The Bible calls this being born again. Are you born again?

Nicodemus asked Jesus a funny question: how can a man be born again when he is old? Will he go back into mom's belly?

Sounds crazy.

But being born again isn't about a second physical birth. That was the first time you were born. Being born again is about being saved.

So, are you saved? Have you been born? Have you been born again? If you've never been born again, you're not saved. Get that taken care of!

I've heard some people say that they've always believed in God, or that they've just... always kind of been saved. But you weren't "always kind of" alive. You were born at some point. You had a birth. That's why you have a birthday.

So when's your birthday?

Think about it. Do you remember the day you got saved? Or do you think you've just always kind of been born... again.

Thank God I had a birthday yesterday. I'm 22 years old. I was 5 when I was born again. What's your story?

We Should Always Be Growing (Spiritually, That Is!) But What's It Look Like?

This note came after the teens had been serving at church...

We should always be growing spiritually.

That's a given. But what does "growing" look like?

Well, whether you see it in yourself or not, spiritual growth is often very evident in you from the outside looking in. Meaning, others might see growth in you that even you don't see yourself.

A few areas that I'm pleased to see spiritual growth in is your **service**. I think back to myself when I was in high school, and I don't remember serving at church near as much as some of you. I appreciate the guys who came down on Friday to just... weed. That's a HUGE help! It's service. It's a blessing. It's a mark of spiritual growth. Willingly serving without expecting to get paid takes amazing spiritual maturity.

Another sign of spiritual growth has been the extra day per week that some of the guys are coming for a **special class.** That's an extra day of emphasis on God's Word. It's a sign of spiritual growth, and it's one of my favorite times in the whole week. Seriously.

One more area is your faithful attendance to **Saturation Saturdays.** I know you don't just come for the food, because we never promise a meal. I know you don't come to just hang out (although that's a fun part!) I know you don't come because you just feel obligated. I believe you come to Saturation Saturday because you love the Lord and want to be obedient to Him. Praise God! That's spiritual growth.

Spiritual growth shows in SO many different ways, from church attendance, to encouraging notes, to your spirit and attitude, to what you post on Facebook. It shows. It's evident.

Even when YOU don't see it, we do. Your youth pastor sees it, and I love it. LOVE it. Praise God for your spiritual growth. That's what life is all about.

What If?

Girls, what if (someday in the FAR future) an amazingly good-looking man asks you to marry him, and he plans on being a missionary... would you be ready?

What are you doing now to prepare?

What if God calls you to preach, men? Would you be ready? What are you doing now to prepare?

What if you're called to be a music director someday? Or what if someday you are a member of a small little country church with no piano player? Would you be ready to serve? What are you doing now to prepare?

What if someone stopped coming to the youth department because no one talked to him or her? What are you doing to make sure that doesn't happen?

What if someone started coming to the Teens of Faith just because you asked them to? Have you tried lately?

What if everyone around you got as mad on the inside as you? Would we have happy people in our lives? What are you doing to work on that?

What if God wanted you to go to Bible college someday? Would you go? What are you doing right now to know His will?

What if God wanted you to return as an intern or someday serve as a church secretary? Would you be spiritually qualified? What are you doing right now that might cause some "red flags?" What are you doing right now that is preparing you?

"What if..." So many "what ifs" in life. You have an uncertain future. All you have is right now. That's all you always will ever have. You will never know the future. So what are you doing now to prepare yourself for the future?

Is Our Church Legalistic? Let's See...

If we teach you that you HAVE to add something to your faith or you're not saved, then, yep... we're legalistic.

If we teach that you're not going to heaven unless you are **baptized**, then we're legalistic. If we teach that you're not saved unless you come to **church**, then we're legalistic. If we teach that you have to read your **Bible** or you go to hell, then we're legalistic.

Legalism—strictly speaking—is adding something to your salvation.

Our mantra is: "Love God, love others, and do right," STARTING with the first and most important: LOVE GOD.

Legalism is about *forcing* you into compliance by threatening you with hell.

Love is about obeying God because you understand... He first loved you. *We love him because he first loved us.*

I feel the need to remind you once again that everything we preach—as hard as it may be sometimes—is NOT legalism. If I preach that drinking is a sin or that every one of you should be reading your Bible... those are not rules you HAVE to follow or else you lose your salvation or something crazy like that. Those are just Bible truths that a Christian who loves God will say, "God, I love you too much to disobey you. I know you want my best, so if drinking is wrong, I won't drink. If your Word is good for me, I love you, and I'll try to hear from you by reading your Word."

Churches that add to the Gospel are legalistic (baptism, sacraments, going on missions, penance, rosaries, giving money...). Churches that preach Bible truths with "loving God" at the center are doing exactly what Jesus did.

So... love God. Love others. Do right.

Oh No! I Lost 'My' Seat!

This note came after we set up our youth room differently...

"Your" seat?

With the chairs being set up a little differently now, you might be sitting in a different place than you normally sit, but no seat was ever "your" seat. Switching things up is good for you. It breaks things up. It freshens things. It gets you out of a rut.

I'm all for routines. I have a morning routine. We have a routine we follow in the offices and during church services. Routines are fine, provided they don't make you a thoughtless robot. If you're in a routine of daily Bible reading, your alarm clock is not what's spiritual ("I'm spiritual because I wake up every day and have my devotions."). Your Bible reading and prayer are the part of the routine that is spiritual. When you routinely come to Sunday morning, Sunday night, and Wednesday night church; the services and the schedule of church is not what's spiritual... worship is spiritual. The preaching is spiritual. The singing is spiritual. The fellowship with others is spiritual.

Don't get stuck in a rut, singing songs out of habit. Sitting in your seat out of habit. Talking only to your friends out of habit.

Break up your routine and think about what we're here to do today. Our youth room is under construction right now, and it will change some more over the next few weeks as we add and remove some things. Let the changes wake you up a little and cause you to think more clearly about what God has for you today.

"Your" seat? No... think about how you can bless others today while focusing on what God has for your life. Who knows... maybe your new seat will wake you up during the preaching a little more. Who knows... maybe God will radically change your life today. Are you open to His call?

Prayer

If prayer is just as big as God is, as the song says, than we as Christians ought to be using it every day. Not as a last resort, but as the first option for everything.

I think a lot of teens are afraid to pray for a lot of reasons. Here are a few:

1) It's too hard to stay consistent

2) I know I'm going to sin again, so what's the use?

3) I don't know what to say / I can't pray very long

4) I feel guilty when I pray

5) It's easier NOT to pray

The list could continue.

In all my years as a youth pastor, I have known very few teens who pray—I mean, REALLY pray. While I'm at it—I've known very few parents who pray! We have created programs that have helped teens read their Bibles, but I know of no good way to consistently track prayer. Then, if it gets tracked, it loses the heart behind the prayer.

This section will encourage you with a few articles on prayer.

Pray Each Day For a Different "Category" of Prayer Request

This note came after a 4-day prayer revival meeting with Evangelist Benny Beckum...

Bro. Beckum emphasized prayer — our talking TO God in that father/child relationship. Have you done that this week?

If you say, "I'm not sure what to pray for. My prayers take, like, 30 seconds, maximum." Set aside the time every day and go through a list and you'll have TOO much to pray for! Or, separate your list into categories each day:

- **Daily** - confess sin, love God, family, thank God, ask for wisdom (Jam 1:5), Armor of God (Eph. 6), God's direction (school today, college future, future husband/wife...), lost people (ACTS method - Adoration, Confession, Thanksgiving, Supplication), yield my members to you...

- **Sunday** - worship (read Psalms, read hymns, talk to God about His greatness, recognize yourself before him (Psalm 19, Isa. 6, Isa. 66:1-2...)

- **Monday** - church (Pastor, Bro. Ryan and Mrs. Jamie, Bakers, TOF members, outreach program, friendships, problems you know about, Sunday school teachers by name, ministries by name and need...)

- **Tuesday** - school (lost friends, saved friends, backslidden friends, teachers, school leadership...)

- **Wednesday** - America (political leaders, state leaders, city leaders, Churches, church planters by name, cities, states, current events...)

- **Thursday** - Colleges (HBBC leadership, college students: *list them by name*)

- **Friday** - Foreign Missions (Pray through missionary cards, website list, weekly missions bulletin, needs, field, God to call you...)

- **Saturday** - Church prayer list (salvations, health needs...), soul winning burden, door knocking today...

I personally pray for places I've been like Heartland, Southwest Baptist Church in OKC, Bible Baptist in Stillwater - all their leaders, my friends, the direction the churches and ministries are going, financial help, special needs, problems...

Anyway... it's a LOT to pray for when you break it down like that! This is just a QUICK list and only IDEAS on how to pray. Come up with your own personal list over time, use it, and you'll grow, grow, grow.

How Long Has It Been?

This note followed an in-your-face sermon on some specific sins...

Last Sunday, the sermon from Leviticus was all about the seriousness of sin.

Awkward...

Why? Because we ALL sin. Me too. And Mrs. Jamie, and Bro. Wilson, and Ms. Sarah, and Pastor...

Need I go on?

So, am I a hypocrite for preaching against sin when ALL the leaders are sinners, too? No. We're all working on this thing together. Paul (the apostle) knew God closer than any of us, yet the Christian walk was a struggle for him, too.

So when you hear about how BAD sin is, and that you—YOU— have sin that offends God, what do we now DO with a sermon like that?

If you don't plan on changing, that's between you and God. God will chasten His children, sooner or later, so it won't be a *fun* road for you.

But, if you're not in-your-face about it and *hateful* against God, and you sin in the general course of life (like ALL of us do), what then?

We're all sinners, but there are a couple different types of sinners:

1. Those who care

2. Those who don't care

Those who don't care (2) won't be into it, anyway, so until God's Spirit gets a hold of their lives and they give in to His conviction, they'll have a rough road. Some of YOU are on that road, and I hurt for you. You haven't read today's announcement sheet, so you won't read me saying this, but **I love you, and want you to surrender to God.** I want to help, if you'll let me.

Those who DO care (1) are going to try to do what God instructs —live by the Spirit, confess and forsake his sin, draw nigh to God, etc. But here's a news flash: you will still sin. *What?! I thought when I surrendered to God, everything would be EASY!* Wrong-o.

So what do you do when you CARE (1), but you still sin?

Same thing as always: confess and forsake. *Yeah, but I've done that.* Do it again. *But I've done it, like a LOT.* Keep it up. Don't stop. Keep the struggle real. Don't give up. Rise yet again. *But I feel like a hypocrite.* At times, we ALL do, because we all sin.

Here are some practical tips to help you that care (1)...

1. **Pray without ceasing.** Like, pray daily, throughout the day. Have a *time* of prayer in the morning, but then as you go through the day, keep God on your mind. *Always* be thinking on God, as if He's right there beside you (He is, btw.)

2. **Read Scripture.** Find something to take with you— one verse, or phrase, or thought. Something—anything —from your Bible. Start small, and grow. It's a love letter, and it will help you.

3. **Be honest.** Maybe it's an accountability partner, maybe it's a friend, maybe it's a leader or a parent. Find a few people who will love you enough to sit beside you and understand. Don't pretend nothing's wrong—we've all lived enough to know that's false!

4. **Get closer to your youth leaders.** I want to help you, and so do the other youth leaders. Some of you have been in "big" trouble and have seen how we still love you unconditionally. "Big" trouble is smaller than you might think. *He'll be so mad. He'll be so*

disappointed. He'll yell at me... Nope. We're shoulder to shoulder WITH you in this.

5. **Consider Christ.** Think about HIS stripes for YOUR sin. Just think. Think about the blood pouring from His head, hands, back, face. Think about those that said He was unrecognizable as a human, or think about the whipping He endured. For you. He knows you best, yet He loves you most.

The song lyrics I read Sunday were so good, here they are again:

How long has it been since you talked with the Lord

And told him your heart's hidden secrets?

How long since you prayed?

How long since you stayed on your knees till the light shone through?

How long has it been since your mind felt at ease?

How long since your heart knew no burden?

Can you call him your friend?

How long has it been since you knew that he cared for you?

How long has it been since you knelt by your bed

And prayed to the Lord up in heaven?

How long since you knew that he'd answer you

And would keep you the long night through?

How long has it been since you woke with the dawn

And felt this day is worth living?

Can you call him your friend?

How long has it been since you knew that he cared for you?

Some Excellent Excuses To Use For Not Writing Postcards (You Can Use These!)

This note was in preparation for special preaching services with Bro. Sam Davison...

Ms. Sarah put the postcards for Bro. Davison in the back of the room. Now you can go to the counter, write a note, and leave it with Ms. Sarah and SHE will mail it for you, if you want.

So there goes a few of THOSE excuses:

- ~~I forgot~~
- ~~I couldn't find the postcards~~
- ~~I didn't know his address~~
- ~~I wasn't sure what to do~~
- ~~I didn't know where to look~~

I think you only have a few excuses left:

- No hablo ingles. *(Don't lie!)*

- My pen is out of ink and there are no other pens in the universe

- My fingers are broken *(but you can dictate to someone else)*

- I think the rapture will happen before the Revival gets here, so it would be a waste of time. I'd rather redeem the time because the days are evil, so I'll pray instead. *(Right.)*

- I get writer's block and I can't think of what to say. *(tell him you're praying for him, and that you're looking forward to having him at our church, and that you hope he has a safe trip, and that you are hoping God speaks to you through the preaching, and that you* *want to donate $1M to him.)*

If you have other, better excuses, let me know and I'll add them to this incredible list.

Serving

Service is an outflow of a walk with God. Christians who love the Lord and love other people will try to serve others in ANY way that they can—even if it is as simple as washing dishes or folding up tables. Serving at church is a simple way to serve God, and God views the servant as the MVP of Christians.

Here are a few notes about serving...

Teen's Arm Severed While Serving Jesus At Local Church

This note came after a teen cut his wrist on a glass table shattering at a church workday (he got stitches)...

Baker was allegedly attacked while serving God at his local church. Photo - courtesy of Ryan Rench's iPhone.

"Apparently, serving the Lord at the local church can be dangerous business!" So said John Baker, a senior in the youth group at Calvary Baptist Church in Temecula.

"There I was, just helping out, when all of a sudden I was attacked by Danny. He tried to cut my hand off with a piece of glass, but I got away."

An incident at the dumpster of Calvary Baptist has detectives wondering what really did happen. Was this really an "accident," as Danny claims, or is there something deeper? Was it something that took place on the Heartland Road Trip? Something about spending 50 hours together in a bus... in one

Detective Bill Rangel commented on the issue, "Our

investigation is currently in progress, but we can neither confirm nor deny that Danny is at fault."

Danny claims the two were "just throwing away a large piece of glass when it broke, hitting John [Baker] in the wrist."

Witnesses say it happened way too fast to tell. "All I heard was John grunt, and then he grabbed his wrist. I turned away because I don't like the sight of blood." Lois and Anneliese Smith, sisters from Chaparral High School, were "a little nervous at the sight of blood" so they couldn't provide Rangel much information.

Meanwhile, as the investigation continues, Baker is recovering with 13 stitches.

"Sometimes, in the Lord's work, He just requires more" said their youth pastor, Ryan Rench. "I'm just mad that God saw fit to let Baker bleed on my truck seatbelt!" Rench's compassionate spirit that he models is overwhelming to his teens, who seem to adore him.

CBCNEWS

Almost all quotations were from Bro. Ryan's head.

God Will Not Be Impressed With How Fast You Can Run

Serving the Lord is the best thing you could do with your time, because it actually means something! I flipped through a sports magazine this morning... our sports world is FULL of dedicated people! They spend HOURS in the gym, getting in shape, getting stronger, getting faster, learning, growing, teaching, training, excelling... for what? They'll get REALLY good, go pro, get famous (or not!), get rich, get old, then die. Sad!

But then what? God won't say, "Man! You were FAST!"

God will say, "Depart from me, I never knew you." I hate that for people. I wish everyone could have the Savior that I have. And that's the point of serving God. Recently, the preacher challenged us to reach others for Christ, and it convicted me of getting SO caught up in this life that I forget about eternal things.

It was great to see a few guys out for the prayer breakfast yesterday, and then to see 9 come to Saturation Saturday yesterday! On top of that, some of those same people stayed for the work day that afternoon! Do you think God overlooks that? I don't think so!

I know some of you were sick, some had to be out of town, some were already busy, some couldn't get a ride, etc., but I hope ALL of you always work to do things that have eternal value. That's what makes life worth living… serving Jesus Christ out of gratitude for what He's done.

A Challenge and a Warning

First, a challenge… Ready? … Greet everyone in the room today. Do it right now. Go.

When you're done, greet everyone else that comes in. And then… do that every week… for the rest of your life. But seriously, at least today, greet everyone in the room. Go. Now to the note…

I don't know if you realize it totally yet, but the greatest person in the youth group is… the greatest servant. So be a servant all the time.

Girls, stay away from a cry-baby boy who's always making excuses for not being able to lift tables or for how hot it is. Guys, stay away from the snobby little girl who is "too good" to get involved in anything or jump in and help wherever it's needed. Always do right. Always look for friends who do right.

Do right. Love God. Love others.

Okay now go greet everyone since you didn't do it earlier. Disobedient little…

Working=Serving

This note came after a teen workday at our church...

You know when the Bible talks about serving, usually it's talking about work.

Did you know that plain ol' work is actually a way to serve the Lord? How cool is that? Picking up leaves, setting up chairs, learning how to drive on church property by Bro. Ryan Driving Services... yep. It's all in the name of serving God!

All those things happened this week, by the way.

Thank you for those of you who stuck around and helped us set up for Roundup Sunday. We had tons of tables to set up and couldn't have done it without you.

And then Sam set up all those chairs — perfectly straight — on Friday. Sam's been coming out on Fridays to help with the yard work. Guess what... that's a way to serve God.

Then yesterday we had Lexi and Lois cutting up onions, and Kelly spent like 3 hours organizing my music closet! It looks amazing in there! Finally, Rodrick "claims" he was working, but he spent all day learning to drive! Just kidding. He DID drive my truck all over, but he did tons of work around here yesterday. That's serving God! And he gets a bonus of community service hours through school too.

All that's to say, keep up the good work. When it's time to work, work! And work hard. Be diligent. Be a hard worker. Be a servant. Don't just take... give! Give through working. If I can sign off on any hours... bonus! But always remember that God's rewards are better than man's, so praise God for letting you serve Him.

Serving — Keep Up the Work, Especially

the GOOD Work

This note followed a particularly good job that the teens did...

Great job serving on Wednesday night. You were amazing.

Not only did you get done with the tables and chairs quickly, but you made sure that you did a good job, too. That says a lot about you.

Don't just serve to serve. "Yeah, I did my good deed for the week. I served. Sure, whatever." NO! Serve with excellence!

Paul says, "...seek that ye may excel to the edifying of the church" in 1 Corinthians. Every bit of work you do in serving the Lord at church should be done with excellence. You should not only do it, but you should do it well.

I walked in on Wednesday night and you pretty much had the whole room done already. Then, when we had to add more rows, no one complained... you just did it! Great job!

On top of that, I looked down each of the rows and they were perfect... I mean, like, perfectly straight. All the chairs were spaced out just right, all the tables were squared up. Perfect. I loved it. Great job.

So, keep up the good work. Not just the good WORK, but the GOOD work.

Wednesday Night Ministries For ALL

This note introduced our teens to Youth Nights in our midweek services...

Pastor has asked us to do something a little different on Wednesday nights.

Starting in a few weeks, we will be involved in some of the Wednesday night specials in church. At least once per month, we will be able to be involved in the music service in some way —some of you more than others. What an opportunity! Let me explain...

Serving in church is an opportunity... not a drudgery. Serving in church brings eternal rewards and is a simple way to be used by God. Sometimes people wish they could "do more for God" when they hear a convicting sermon. They say, "I want to serve God with my life" but they think that means, like, future-life-some-day-sort-of-when-I'm-like-grown-up life.

When does that life start? When you're 18? 20? 25? 35? 50?

Why not now? Let me help you... it DOES start now!

With the new opportunities to serve on Wednesday nights, you are literally serving the Lord by leading singing, playing the piano, and even being involved in the monthly youth nights in the Wednesday services.

Soon, we will begin asking some of you guys to lead singing (*gasp of terror!) I'll work with you... I promise.

It will be a terrible, horrible, death sentence to you... if you view it that way. But if you view it the right way (i.e. that you are able to biblically serve the Lord!), then leading singing, playing the piano, etc., is an opportunity! It should be, "Thank you, God, for giving me the chance to serve you."

When you're asked to sign up, don't roll your eyes and say, "Uuugh.. okay. Is it only one time I have to do this?" That stinks.

Rather, say, "I might wet my pants I'm so scared, but if I can serve God, I'll do it! If He's willing to use me, I'm willing to be used!" That's the spirit.

Oh, and by the way, leading singing is only one example. If you play the piano or otherwise need to miss our game time, don't worry about it. Our Wednesday night game time is NOTHING compared to what you get to do in being involved in the music. Thank God you get to serve.

Youth Nights Are About God — Not You

I pray you serve out of a heart that loves God.

That's what it's all about.

I'm not trying to knock you down or hurt your feelings, but it's not about you. Singing a special, leading songs, ushering, greeting, or even preaching—these things are not about the person. They are about the God of the person.

If you can grasp that concept and make it real to yourself, you're set for life, spiritually. You will never have major setbacks in your spiritual life if you live by the concepts we've been talking about in Sunday school and Wednesday night classes: love God, love others, and do right.

Bro. Ken and Mrs. Gina's driving motivation at all times was love—loving God with all their hearts so that it overflowed into a love for you. Their example is what the Teens of Faith is all about. My desire is that you see people like the Bakers and Myers as people you can strive to be like someday. I want you to see them for what they are trying to be. Are they perfect? No! God never demands perfection, but He does desire love.

If you can love God with all your heart, soul, mind and strength, you will serve Him correctly. With the Bakers, it was all about serving God and not about the Bakers' glory. Is it that way with you when you're asked to serve on youth nights? Do you sing, preach, usher or greet so that YOU get noticed? If so, realign yourself. Stop. Slow down. Turn around. Do whatever you need to get right with God, and serve Him in love.

Witness Is Here To Empty Their Cups

On this Sunday, the ensemble Witness! from Heartland Baptist Bible College was in our class...

Today in Sunday school we have Witness! all to ourselves. You're a bunch of Witness-hogs! Don't misread that and think I'm calling them hogs... I'm saying you're hogging them. You already got to hang out with them on Friday at Pastor's house, and now today they'll be singing and preaching for us.

I'm excited to have them today. I appreciate their kindness and their ministry. I'm glad they're not all weirdos! They've been at 4 camps this summer, and I am sure they're tired. I remember being tired when I was in their place!

I was listening to a ministry podcast this week that gave the analogy of emptying your cup to try to help others. As you minister, you will never be able to fill other people's cups, but you can empty yours by giving all of yourself. That's the idea of Witness! being with us this weekend. They're not here to recruit or meet every need. Their preaching and singing today is not going to fill everyone's cup and cause a great revival in our church. The filling of your cup is not up to them. The idea is that they are here to empty their cups. They're just here to give. They're singing today with all their energy. They ministered the last few days because they love you. They gave of themselves in volleyball, door-knocking and working at the church because they are here to serve and be a blessing. They're here to empty their cups.

If you see their testimony and like what Heartland is about, that is up to you. If you sense God calling you to Heartland because of the example of the students from there, that is between you and God. Witness! is not here to "twist your arm" and get you to fill out a registration form. They're not competing with each other on how many information packets they can get teens to sign up for, and there's no contest to see who can get the most high-schoolers to go to Heartland. That's not what the tour groups are about. They're here to serve and give. They are here to model the spirit of a lot of the students at Heartland. If you like their spirit and want to be like that yourself, consider going to Heartland.

I Love It When You're Late

Pastor started having special music provided by the teens for our midweek services, and I wrote this note to encourage this ministry...

I love it when you come in really late on Wednesday nights.

Wait, what?! Yep. I love it.

Most of the time, it means you were just serving. Sometimes you're late because you were picking your nose or something. Most of the time, however, it means you were playing or singing the special in church.

I love that.

Every time someone comes in late after singing a special, I smile really big and feel so proud of them. If it was you, you can be sure I was praising God for your service that night.

Church is the best place to use your talents. God is the one who gave you the talents, anyway... So use them for Him! He gave them to you, He empowers you in using them, and then He blesses you for using them. How cool is that?!

I love the Lord, and I love when you serve Him.

Keep coming in late. But only if you're serving God.

Two Opportunities For Serving

Sometimes the church has specific needs that need to be kept in an eternal perspective...

Service is at the heart of God. Life as a Christian is about others, not self, so serving others is how to focus your attention on others. It's not just about thinking about others, but actually about doing things to help others.

You can serve God by serving others. Many of you are great servants. Keep up the good work.

Sometimes, though, you are not always sure where to serve. Here are a couple suggestions:

Weekly class setup. If you are able and interested, I need someone who will become the person to set up the tables for the ladies Bible study. Every Wednesday it needs to be set up a certain way. If you are interested in an area in which you can be faithful, please let me know. It is too hard for most of you, I know. But the one (or two) who is willing will be serving God.

Wash chalkboard. I would like the chalkboard washed each week. It takes about 5-7 minutes with a sponge-mop. It is a simple job that can be done maybe Wednesday nights after church, Sunday nights after church, Saturdays after door-knocking, or any other time in the week.

Serving God is usually plain ol' work. Let me know if you are able to help in this way. I'm excited to see who's first to volunteer.

Workdays Aren't Supposed To Be Fun

This note came after a church workday...

A bunch of you were out at yesterday's workday, and the church looks great! It was a blessing to see you all working so hard. It's almost not fair when you're actually having fun! It's supposed to be work, right?! Who says God's people and God's work isn't fun? I have the best job in the world, and working at church is exactly God's design for you. No wonder it's fun.

Hard Workers. I Like It. It's Eternal.

This note came after a church workday...

Even some of you ladies who were going to a bridal shower were still at the workday yesterday... I like it! Great work.

A *bunch* of you showed up yesterday for the workday. We had pretty much everyone busy the whole time, and we STILL didn't get all the weeding done. At least we got most of the trees hacked and the flower beds up front all cleared out. Oh, and a couple guys changed all the attic filters. That's a fun job!

If you were here yesterday, you were serving God. You might think, "No I wasn't... I was pulling weeds and picking up sticks. Big deal."

It IS a big deal. It's eternal. You were serving at church for a purpose larger than you. I feel bad for those who couldn't come yesterday. I feel even worse for those who didn't *want* to come. That's a heart condition. That's a character that needs to be changed. *Not* wanting to work means there's *not* a fear of God in the heart.

This past week I worked through the entire book of Proverbs and pulled out every verse about money. You know what I found out? A lot of the areas it talks about making money, it also talked about diligence and hard work. Hmm... are you seeing what I'm seeing?

There's a direct correlation between hard work and God's blessings. Sure, we say it's just about "spiritual" hard work like reading your Bible and praying. But that's not all. Hard work—even "spiritual" hard work—still looks like... work. Like... weeding, picking up sticks and filling the dumpster.

Good job serving God yesterday. That's what life should be all about. Love God, love others, and do right.

Be Obsessive About Your Service To the King

A large part of the Christian life is serving God.

Tonight, you had one more opportunity to serve your King. If you call Him LORD, is He? Does he really rule your life, like a lord rules a kingdom?

God should.

Being the Lord's "subject" ought to change you.

It ought to make you want everything to be perfect for the King.

I'm a little obsessive about certain things. There are some projects I completely forget about, but others that I go super crazy on. For example, Lexi, today, came to work in the music closet. It drives me crazy that it's not perfect. I need every song in those drawers to be in number order. I need to know exactly how many sheets of music we have for each song. I need to know the composer, arranger and publisher of every song. I need to know everything! So, Lexi was in there all afternoon sorting those songs, putting them in numerical order and reporting on how many are missing.

Another obsessive example—researching new hymnals. Since ours are out of print, we need a hymnal with all our current favorite hymns *and* one that includes orchestration. So, we gathered up all our songbooks, sorted through the song lists in the back and then printed the NEW hymnals' song lists. Then, we went through every single song title to see if OUR hymns were in the NEW hymnal, and wrote down the song titles that were missing. Finally, we compared the new hymnals to each other to see which ones had the most and the best songs.

It was kind of a crazy project. I mean, most normal people would have kind of just looked at the new hymnals and figured, "Yep. This one has 900 songs in it. I bet it is a good one!"

I guess we could have done that, too. But, like I said, I'm a bit obsessive about certain projects, and this was one of them.

We try to do that on purpose, though. We want to be thorough in our service to the King. We want to make sure we're using our finances wisely. We want to make sure we're making the right and the best choice of hymnals. If our song service is so essential to our worship of God, then we want to have thought through as many of the small details as possible.

I love my King. I want things to be perfect for Him.

Do you serve Him out of a deep respect and love? Do you get obsessive about serving Him?

Don't get sloppy with ushering, singing, or greeting. Serve the King well by getting a little bit obsessive. I'm sure others will understand.

Youth Night Song Leader Story
[Interactive Story]

Once upon a time there was a class full of people your age, calling themselves the Teens of Faith, meeting in a room just like this one. You are one of them. You quite enjoy it.

One day, the youth pastor announces that there is a Youth Night coming up, and that he needs a volunteer song-leader.

You get nervous. "I hope he doesn't call on me," you think.

Do you:

> Hide behind your announcement sheet? (GO TO 10)
>
> Shift in your seat and avoid eye contact? (GO TO 15)
>
> Gulp and raise your hand to volunteer? (GO TO 30)

This story originally appeared in the teen announcement sheets, and they followed a series of choices taped to the walls. To Read the short interactive story, visit RyanRench.com/ TOFStory.

Thank You To All Who Serve

I want to encourage those who serve. Here are some specific instances of service...

You do a lot around here.

I love it.

After the ladies meeting last Friday, my wife came home raving about how well you ladies did serving. You saw the need and did whatever jobs were waiting. I love that.

And your great service in reaching out to guests... that's wonderful. Some of you go out of your way to be *extra* friendly —talking with the guest, welcoming them, showing them where to sit, etc.—I think that's great. Even though it's awkward meeting new people, I appreciate those of you who push past your nerves and go do what you should. You are so friendly, and I would love that to spread to others, too. Thank you—those of you who do this—for being the leader and the servant in this area.

Also, thank you to those who do periodic jobs, like Alexa scheduling games and Anastasia setting up chairs (ladies Bible study) and posting things on the website. And Michael C. doing the missionary videos whenever we have one, and all of you setting up tables last week. I really appreciate all those little things. That says a lot about you.

I know I miss things all the time. I know there are more ministries that you're involved in—nursery, Jr. church, choir, and more that are also weekly—but I appreciate the thoughtful, intentional moments that I see you serving outside of yourself, investing in others.

It's the simple things that make me happy. Seeing you greet others in church. Seeing you branch out of your friend groups to others. Seeing you welcome and include new people. Seeing you smile. Seeing you sing during congregationals.

I love those things. Thank you. Great work.

Music

Our church's music is intentionally traditional. We use hymns on purpose and encourage total separation from the world in church and personal music. It is not like we are stuck in the 1950's or anything like that. I like new music as much as the next guy.

It's more that I want to be holy in all areas of life and please God with what goes in my ears and comes out of my mouth. Music is a powerful tool for good or bad, and I appreciate those teens who take a stand against the culture to only allow godly influences into their lives through their music.

Here are a couple notes that helped encourage our teens...

I Used To Be Embarrassed About Listening To Good Music

This note was from the week our church hosted the Assurance Trio from Heartland Baptist Bible College...

Tonight we get to hear the Assurance Trio from Heartland. I'm excited to get to know this group and hear their good music.

I thought the Cepeda special on Wednesday was awesome. How does that relate to Assurance Trio? Well, they had the music memorized and sang the song well, in part because they'd listened to the song so many times. I know they worked hard on the song because it takes a while to memorize a song. But... It's a lot easier to do when you LISTEN to the music.

What kind of music do you listen to? Don't ever be embarrassed to say that you listen to conservative, Christian music. It used to be a common question for me when I was in high school: "What kind of music do you listen to?" I used to hem-haw around because I was a little embarrassed about my music. If I listened to anything, it certainly wasn't what the "cool" people listened to.

Now, I'm GLAD to say that I listen to godly Christian music that helps me, spiritually. How about you?

If you don't "like" good Christian music, then change your "likes." Learn to love the right things and you will be blessed. Start tonight. Buy some good CDs and start listening to good music! You'll be pleased, eventually, I promise!

Get GOD'S Idea For Your Music

With all this new stuff I've been working on with choir, I've become more and more passionate about music.

God's idea about music.

Lots of people have their ideas. I want God's.

There's a big difference. "Nah. Music is no big deal. It doesn't affect me." Well, tonight I hope you'll see it DOES affect you. You can't help it!

If it's wrong, ditch it. If it's right and righteous before God, get as much as you can of it!

A Couple Life Lessons Today

First lesson—ask good questions before diving into a project.

I had an opportunity presented to me for a fundraiser for our group. It would have been a great chance to earn a lot of money. Unfortunately, the fundraiser included selling discounts to various wineries and pubs, among other businesses.

I should have asked. I should have known what we'd be selling before agreeing to accept the fundraiser. No hard feelings on either end, though. Thankfully, we did not lose money on the transaction.

An additional lesson for you is to *never*—under any circumstances—compromise your beliefs for money. The Bible is very clear about drinking. We don't want anything to do with that, so we are not going to sell discount cards to wineries (even when it would have been PURE profit for us).

Another lesson came when I was browsing the radio. An audiobook I was listening to made me wonder what the radio airwaves were playing, so I flipped it on in my truck. One of the first songs that caught my attention (once I finally figured out which button changed the station!) was the "By Faith" song we sang at camp.

I have nothing against the song. I have nothing against the words. I hope that's obvious (we sang it as our camp song in church the Sunday after camp last year, remember?).

What I AM against is the performance I heard. I guess I was hearing the original version. It was full on CCM (contemporary Christian music)—a mixture of pop and rock, sort of. Did it draw me into the words? Nope. Did it deepen my love for God? No, it didn't. Did it stir me to live a life of faith? No. I was concentrating on other things. Things like the performer's voice and the rhythm made me lose the depth. It sounded like every other secular song I bounced past. There was nothing distinctly "Christian" about it except the words.

I thought Christian music was supposed to be... Christian. Christ is UNLIKE everything secular and worldly.

The Bible teaches us to be clearly holy—set apart.

One of my main issues with CCM is what I experienced as I scanned the radio. I heard a song I had become familiar with in another venue, so I stopped and listened.

The book *The Power of Habit* explains that the music industry teaches you to like certain songs. Your brain likes certain music because it is trained to—over a period of time you develop a habit of music tastes.

CCM tries to blend two worlds that shouldn't be together.

When we sing songs like "By Faith" in a church setting, I hope you are mature enough to know that music is MUCH more than lyrics. FAR more goes into a song than you realize, and the *way* it is sung has as much to do with the message as the lyrics themselves.

Stay away from CCM. Even if it's a song you have heard in our church, that doesn't mean everyone who sings it is doing it with pure and godly motives and methods. Good songs can be sung in bad ways, defeating the whole purpose.

That was a little life lesson for me—be very careful what I allow into my heart. I might create a craving for the music *style* more than the *truth* itself.

Philosophies & Reasons

My preaching tends to default to a reasoning/philosophical style. I like to figure out WHY we do what we do.

Some of my favorite preachers are more of what I call "Conference Style" preachers. They can tell incredible stories, sway your heart, and powerfully communicate the simplest of truths.

I wish I could be like them. Oh, I wish, I wish I wish! I see so much value in that, and I work to BE that for my teens.

However, if I get good at swaying people's emotions, I had better have reasons WHY I teach and preach my content. I need to know and be able to articulate why we do what we do, so I try to teach our teens that there is a reason behind everything we do in our youth ministry.

This section describes a couple of these philosophical notes...

Testimonies. Why Do Them? A Philosophy Of Sharing Our Heart Out Loud.

At last week's campfire we had a time of testimonies. Testimonies are a good thing to be involved in.

Testimonies encourage others. Whether you realize it or not, your testimonies are a huge encouragement to me and others. For me, it is awesome to hear that God is working in your lives through the preaching, and it is validating to feel like I'm not wasting my time spending 4 or 5 hours on Sunday mornings putting the final touches on the sermons. I can go a long time on a few key testimonies and encouragements. Also, your testimonies encourage others to speak up too. Did you notice how a lot of our testimonies went along with others? Hearing others' struggles and victories is always a help to you, right? So be a part of testimonies if we have them, and encourage others.

Testimonies help you be accountable. You don't want to look like a liar if you give a testimony about being a better example at school and then never do anything about it. Speaking up at a testimony time helps people see where your heart is, but it also gives them an expectation of what to look for in you.

Testimonies help you make concrete decisions. Application days should be specific and actionable. You should be able to put a little checkbox by most of your decisions and check it off as "done" when you act on Bible preaching. When you make a decision on your own and don't share it with anyone, sometimes it's hard to actually do anything about it because it isn't totally clear even to you. You know you were convicted about... something... but you can't really remember what. Ever been there? I have. Testimony times help you articulate your thoughts and put into words what you're sensing from God. When you can speak it or write it, it will be much easier to act on.

Is Christ Prominent or Preeminent?

When Christ is *prominent* in a person's life, others *might* notice. Maybe there's a Scripture verse hanging on the wall of his office, or maybe there's a Christian fish on the back of her car.

Those are okay, but incomplete.

When Christ is *preeminent* in a person's life, it is unmistakable.

Pastor preached from Colossians last Sunday about Christ not merely being prominent—visible and up front—but being *preeminent*—being *everything* to you as a Christian.

Your relationship to Christ can only be cultivated by a deepening relationship with the Word.

In the beginning was the Word, and the Word was with God, and the Word was God.

Christ exists in His Word, and you draw closer to God by becoming intimately closer to His Word.

The Christian with only a *Prominent Christ* might miss a day or two (or week, or month...) of Bible reading, and it might not bother him.

The Christian with a *Preeminent Christ* cannot miss a day of Bible reading. To this Christian, a day away from his Bible is an entire 24 hours apart from his Christ—his Friend, Father, Companion, Comforter, and his Everything.

The Christian with only a *Prominent Christ* might read the Scriptures out of duty. He might read with only a surface understanding. He might be glad he completed his day's assigned reading. He might understand less than 10% of what he read, yet does not seem to care. He feels that he has faithfully read, therefore he must be okay.

The Christian with a *Preeminent Christ* has to know the Christ of the Scriptures. He reads not merely to read about, but to *know* God. He reads to find God's thoughts. He reads to understand. He reads to change. He reads to grow. He *must* know what God said, so that he can then know what God is saying still today. Since Christ is *everything* to him, it is not enough to know a few things about him (i.e. the details of the virgin birth, his blood atonement, the parables he taught, etc.), but to *know Him*.

Which view of Christ do you have?

Encouragement

I keep encouragement files of all kinds: physical (all the notes and cards I have received), email (label: "Encouragements") and text (copied to an Evernote file). I appreciate the times that people have encouraged me, and I want to help others do the same.

Encouragement is an important subject in the Teens of Faith. These articles were encouraging encouragements to encourage!

Have You Encouraged Anyone This Week?

Have you helped anyone?

Have you shared the gospel?

Have you been a good testimony at school?

Have you posted ONLY good stuff this week?

My wife sent me an article basically saying that social media will pretty much know more about you than YOU know about you. Someday you'll look back at things you posted and say, "Did I REALLY say that?! That's embarrassing!"

Someday, you'll give account to God of everything you say and do. Social media only makes you give account of what you type, "like," or upload. How much of it (just this week!) has been spiritually beneficial to anyone?

I'm not accusing, because I don't know the answer to that question. God does. And you do.

Love God. Post good stuff about others. Do right.

Be An Encourager, and You'll Never Be Short Of Friends

This note came after a particularly encouraging week...

LAST FRIDAY we had a very encouraging time around the campfire as you gave testimonies and challenged each other to live for Christ. THE NEXT DAY there were lots of you out for soul-winning, and we got to spend time with our favorite people in the church... you. Sundays are always encouraging for me because we're around each other and in God's Word, but LAST SUNDAY was especially encouraging because someone that Bro. Bagley and Tyler invited on door-knocking came to church! The most encouraging part... Tyler didn't scare them away!!

ON MONDAY AND TUESDAY I got to spend some time thinking about the Teens of Faith's past and future, and I'm always encouraged to think about where most of you have come over the last year and where I dream for us to be with this next series coming up. THIS COMING SUNDAY you'll hear more about the series, but I promise right now that all of you will benefit from it if you're open to the learning and the change God desires to bring in you.

DIScouragement is a sin brought about from wrong thinking (Num. 21:1-7), and we can sure do a lot better at staying ENcouraged every day. David encouraged himself in the Lord. Even when no one else is there to lift you up, know that God has given you plenty to be thankful for.

A lesson there: encourage others. Be an encouragement somehow this week. Be an encourager your whole life, and you'll never have need of friends.

Godly Friends Encourage Each Other To BE Godly By BEING Godly

This note came after I was encouraged by my friends when we were together at a conference...

How often do you encourage one another? You might do it without even realizing it.

I got to spend time with some of my best friends last week. Bro. John Lande was my best friend in college, and continues to be an encouragement to me. When I was in OKC last week, we sat by each other during all the services and messed around the whole time (shame on us). When we went out to eat, Bro. Lande sat next to Mrs. Cepeda and she was wondering what our connection was, asking if we went to college together. We told her, "No, we just met," but she knew it was a lie. We were too crazy together.

Being around my friends encourages me. It's fun. I have a good time. I'm challenged by them. I want to be like them. I want to have the testimony that Bro. Lande has with his life.

On Wednesday night after church, I was invited out to eat by my other friend—Seth Bailey—the youth pastor at Southwest Baptist in OKC. He has another friend from El Paso whom I was introduced to, and I was encouraged by these men, as well. We talked about youth ministry (go figure, right?) through the whole dinner, and I was challenged and encouraged by their ministries. I wanted to be and do more for God because of them.

Spiritual friendship is not all about talking spiritual all the time. It might just be about encouraging one another. So what about you? Have you been encouraged by your friends lately? Have you encouraged each other this week? Love God, love others, and do right. That will be encouraging in itself. Godly friends encourage each other to BE godly by BEING godly.

Whatever Happens, Be Encouraging By Participating

One of the most encouraging things you can do is to participate.

Anyone can sit out. Anyone can laugh at others. Anyone can

think, "This is stupid." Anyone can smirk. Anyone can say, "Psh." Anyone can be negative.

Don't be "anyone."

Be encouraging. Be positive. Be nice. Be uplifting.

And be intentional. You should be encouraging *on purpose.*

Which means... here's a *really* practical and real-life example... get involved in whatever game we do tonight. Decide *right now* that it will be a great game time, and that you'll have a good time. I mean, seriously—stop reading and think this to yourself, *"I'm going to love it tonight, whatever it is."*

You can be more of an encouragement than you realize when you just stop being negative.

When it's your turn to run a game, you'll appreciate the people who dive in there as volunteers. You'll appreciate the people who aren't snickering or muttering things under their breath to their friends. You'll appreciate the people who don't point at you and laugh. You'll appreciate the people who say, "Thanks for doing that game. It was fun!" You'll appreciate the encouragers. (The same goes for those of you who will lead singing on youth night, give a testimony in church, preach in class, etc.) You'll focus on the distracting people, and you'll get self-conscious about the people who are laughing or aren't having a good time.

Forget them, though. Forget the discouragers. They need to realize that <u>fun is what you make it</u>.

So *choose* right now to have fun. Choose to be an encourager. The games will *never* be lame—even if it's a lame game—as long as YOU choose for them to be fun.

Resurrection

The foundation of our Christianity rests in the resurrection. Almost every year around Easter I try to revisit the topic of the resurrection and remind our teens why we meet weekly on Sundays.

Today's Easter. In Case You Were Wondering.

Oooooh! Thanks so much for that, Bro. Ryan. I wasn't sure.

Sure, no problem. I hope you enjoy your day with family, digging in to all your candy. (By the way, my wife gave me an Easter BUCKET... not just a basket this morning! Jelly Beans, a solid white chocolate bunny, gummy bears and more... I love my wife. She gives me candy.)

But more than the candy and all the weird guys dressed up in scary bunny suits, remember the full reason for being here today. Lots of people attend church on Easter because of the importance of what it stands for, and I hope you let that level of importance affect you. Dwell on Christ's resurrection today. Let it sink in. Listen during the messages, and ask God to change your heart. Let him challenge your lifestyle, and do what He tells you today.

What a privilege it is to be in church today. I hope God speaks to you through the services, and I pray you have a blessed day. Do right.

Church Is a Weekly Celebration Of the

Resurrection

Without the resurrection, we'd all be wasting our time here today.

Read 1 Cor. 15 sometime and you'll see what I mean. Paul basically said that everything he ever lived for would have been worthless if it wasn't for the resurrection.

The fact that Christ has power over death is what makes Christianity unique. The fact that Christ rose from the dead is what separates us from religions. Catholics still have Christ on the cross, and they worship his mother. Muslims can visit their founder's grave and find bones. Buddhists have a statue of their dead leader. We visit Christ's tomb and it's empty!

You may have heard it a million times, but never let Christ's resurrection get old. We "celebrate" his resurrection as we meet together on the first day of each week—the day of his resurrection and the day they met for church in the Bible (that's why we don't do Saturday services). Christ's resurrection drives everything that we do, and one day we will be resurrected with him. Overwhelming.

This Is THE Difference Between Christianity and Religion

The different between Christianity and every religion out there is that our Savior is risen.

And the crazy thing is... He raised Himself!

Muhammad couldn't do that. Joseph Smith couldn't do that. Confucius couldn't do that. The fake created being that Mormons call "Jesus" couldn't raise himself. Even Catholics, who claim to be Christians, still have Jesus on the cross. They believe more in Mary and in their good works than they do in God!

How'd Jesus do that? How did He raise... Himself?!

Only one person has power over death. God! He created life, so He has ALL power over life. You're alive because of God.

So how did Jesus—who was dead—raise Himself from the dead?!

There's only one answer... He is God. Jesus had power over death because He was and is God.

Get this... WE have power over death because WE are given that same power! Everything we do and live for as Christians is because we serve a risen Savior who has promised us that same resurrection power that He has.

If you're not saved, you have no power over death. Your body will die, and then God's judgment for ALL your sins will be poured out on you. Have you ever lied? Then you're a liar, right? Have you ever stolen? Then you're a thief, right? How about taking God's name in vain? That's blasphemy, and it's very serious to God. If you've ever said, "Oh my God" is an improper way (not actually reverent to God), then you're a blasphemer. Oh yeah... AND you're a lying, thieving blasphemer. When God judges you, how will you do? Pass or fail?

If you fail, you'll die twice. Your body dies, then your spirit dies.

The cool part is, if you become a Christian (obey what the Bible says to be saved from your sin), you only die once, but then you receive God's resurrection power! You don't have to fear death (or God's judgment after that) because Jesus conquered death and offers you HIS power.

God's judgment isn't something I'd EVER want to face. You CAN avoid it. Jesus died and rose again just for you. He died for your sin and rose to conquer your sin. All you have to do is accept Him as Lord and repent of that sin. If you have never done that, let us show you how today! Seriously! We want to help you.

Every Sunday, Be Intentional About

Celebrating This

Every Sunday is a celebration of one thing: the resurrection of Jesus Christ.

It would be a sad, sad religion to have no hope of anything except MY good works and MY tithing and MY being a good person and MY work... That's a lot of stress on ME.

Thankfully, Christianity isn't about DOING anything, because it's not about ME! True Christianity is about believing in and completely trusting a resurrected Savior—Jesus Christ.

So, every Sunday around here is a celebration of Jesus Christ. That's where the whole "church" thing came from, anyway. To meet on a Sunday is to celebrate the resurrection of Jesus. He arose on a Sunday and then the church started to meet every Sunday as the day of worship.

That's what we do every Sunday.

Do you come to church to celebrate Jesus Christ? He's the only one worth celebrating. Calvary Baptist Church is not about Pastor Rench, it's not about the buildings, and it's not about the attendance. It's not even about you.

It's all about Jesus Christ.

Jesus is the only reason we have to live. He should be everything to you. If He's not, you don't know what you're missing! Turn to Him today!

Cultural Topics

Culture tries to demolish biblical standards. At times, hot topics in the news might cause me to write a biblical perspective. These two notes cover abortion, divorce and homosexuality.

Tough Conversations About Abortion

Have you ever had tough conversations about abortion?

Your friends or teacher might present some compelling arguments in favor of abortion, but is it ever right?

No way, Bro. Ryan!

You might think *"No way!"* ...but could you argue it? If it were a debate topic in your speech class, would you have a good argument?

I just watched one of the most AMAZING videos that ALL of you should watch! It's on YouTube as "180 movie."

A man named Ray Comfort has put together a series of interviews in a compelling 30 minute video, and I'd encourage all of you to search it out and think through what he's talking about. Beyond the issues of abortion, he presents a very cool way to present the gospel: get people to realize their need because of their sin, explain the payment of the cross, and ask for a decision (you'll see what I mean when you watch it.) Have a great week!

[Disclaimer: while I do not agree with everything Bro. Comfort says or does, I appreciate his passion and his spirit.]

Some Things CAN'T Be Optional,

Especially These 2

When Mrs. Jamie and I were going through pre-marital counseling in preparation for our marriage, the counselor said something that stood out to me.

"Ryan and Jamie, you might be totally in love right now, but even though the end is the farthest thing from your minds right now, you still have to purpose right now that this will never end." Sure, of course, we both thought. We are totally in love and cannot wait to get married. Until death do us part and all that.

We both agreed to his statement, but he reiterated it. "You have to decide right now that divorce can never be an option." It struck home. I had never really thought about it, because I had obviously never been in that situation, but it was an impactful time for me. It helped me see that some decisions have to be made now, and they can't be optional. For some reason, these two areas are on my mind for you to think about right now:

Divorce. Divorce should NEVER even be a consideration for you. You need to choose right now that you will never get a divorce. How do you make that decision now? Well, the BEST way is to get it right the first time. Marry a Christian. Marry a devoted Christian, and be that to your future spouse. Right now. Be a devoted Christian.

Homosexuality. Another lifestyle that can never be an option to you is homosexuality. Choose right now that you will never let it creep into your life. Same-sex attraction is real. The world will tell you over and over and over and over and over that it is normal, natural, and okay with God. It is not. It can never be optional. Talk to someone and get it taken care of as sin, and decide now to never let it get a foothold.

Preaching

I love preaching.

I love TO preach, and I love HEARING preaching.

I liked it in high school, but got a passion for it when my friends would bump the preaching tapes LOUDLY in their cars when we were on our way to 6 Flags. We would have revival meetings right there in the back seat, whooping and shouting "Amen!" at everything. That is when I learned to LOVE preaching.

And I want that kind of love for my teens, too.

Yet I also want to teach them to know what GOOD preaching is, too. If I can't always exemplify it through my own preaching, I try to write about it, as you will see in the following notes...

Learn to Recognize Good Preaching As BIBLE Preaching

I went to Heartland last week, and the whole week's preaching was on... Biblical Preaching! I loved it! The Monday evening service was a dedication service for the brand new preaching auditorium on campus, which they named the "Biblical Preaching Center," and Bro. Sam Davison preached the service.

I hope you never take the Bible for granted, and I hope you develop a passion for clear, true, BIBLE preaching. Don't waste my time with motivational talks or "sharing." For that matter, don't waste my time by just reading one little verse and then yelling for the next hour and calling it Bible preaching.

Have you ever written someone a letter? A nice, meaningful, long letter? You put time into it and choose your words carefully. Or have you ever written a 5-page report? You have a goal in mind and you write arguments and develop thoughts throughout your paper.

The Bible is the same way, and it's not meant to just grab a sentence here or there. It's a letter with thoughts, and arguments, and reasons for each sentence. Bible preaching will emphasize 1) What God SAID (to them), and 2) What God is SAYING to you. Learn to discern between weak preaching, springboard preaching, and Bible preaching.

Revival Is Normal

Bro. Billy Ingram preached all last week on revival. The progression of the week was that revival living is normal, and if you're a backsliding heifer then 1) break up your fallow ground, 2) stop your unbelief, 3) recognize you're a nobody from nowhere with nothing and 4) rely on God!

Did you do that this week?

Looking For Ways To Get More Out Of Preaching? Write Something Down.

This note came a week after a sermon on working diligently in YOUR work...

Many of you take notes during the preaching. That is really good. You're paying attention.

But what do you do with those notes? What do you do on Monday before school? Or during school? Or after school? Do you DO anything with the preaching?

Application is how to make the Bible real. If you are only a hearer of the Word and not a doer, you're fooling yourself (the Bible word is *deceiving* yourself. Same thing.).

Are you deceived right now?

Yes or no? How do you know? James 1:22 says that we should

be doers of the word, and not hearers only, or else we are deceiving ourselves. We are fooling ourselves.

So how can you make sure you are not tricked? How can we prepare ourselves for the devil's tricks?

Here's how: DO the Word. When you hear (or read) the Word, do something about it.

For example: working hard. Since last Sunday, have you worked?

And... have you been diligent in YOUR work (chores, pets, school, sports, etc.)? How has YOUR work improved this last week?

If you take notes during class or church, here is an idea for the close of your notes: write down a DO statement. How can you be a DOER of the Word, and not a hearer only?

You will change the way you listen to preaching if you are writing down a simple DO statement at the end. Even if the statement is simple, like, "I plan to make my bed every day this week without being told." Or, "I plan to thank God every day this week for some new part of creation." If it is something related to the preaching, write it down and do it.

If preaching is boring to you, maybe you are deceived. You won't know unless you DO something.

We Are Into Building a Spiritual Environment

On Wednesday, I tried to explain why our church is so focused on preaching the Word of God. I tried to show why our youth ministry is more about the Bible than it is about anything else.

Do we build relationships? Yep. We do a lot of fun things together that build relationships. We work to spend time together. Do we have fun? Yep! You make everything we do together fun. I have a *blast* in youth ministry. There's never been a job title that has matched what a youth pastor gets to do

—organize games, activities, events, trips... we've done a lot of fun things. We have made a ton of memories together.

Memories last only so long, though. When you are old, you may or may not remember the youth water activity or the Knott's Berry Farm trips. You may or may not remember your youth pastor or his kids. BUT... that's not what I am after in youth ministry.

I don't care if you remember me, my wife, my kids, or our events or activities. My MAIN goal is that you get to know God.

I'm bummed about the graduates who leave and get into drinking, into immoral lifestyles or into selfish living. Bummed. But I hope they remember that we had a class who tried to motivate, inspire, and direct them to love God more and more through His Word.

Our youth department is about building a *spiritual* environment. That's what church is all about. That's what the youth ministry should be about. We are not a *separate* thing from the church... we are church members! YOU are, if you are saved and baptized. As a church member, YOUR growth is dependent on the same things as any adult—the preaching of God's Word.

Why do we focus on preaching? Because that's what Paul told Timothy was the best thing for each church member. Why do we have preaching in Sunday school, Sunday morning, Sunday night and Wednesday night services? Because that seems to be God's best church-growth model. Let's all get more into the preaching today.

8 Tips To Encourage the Preaching In Our Church

How's your response to preaching. Here are some REALLY practical things you can do when it's preaching time at our church (in here and in the main services).

Bring your Bible. How about starting there? Bring your Bible to church. And use it! You will never get anything from the preaching if you do not bring your Bible, so make it a point to contribute to the preaching by having your Bible. It's not funny when you forget it. Don't laugh it off. For your sake, God's sake, and others' sake, get serious about God's Word.

Say "Amen." You can contribute to being timeless by saying "Amen" in church. It's a Bible principle to agree and affirm the preaching. The first time you do it you'll feel weird. Keep it up! You will encourage everyone around you.

Stay Awake. Hopefully it goes without saying... you are a discourager—not an encourager—when you are falling asleep during the preaching. Are you passionate about preaching? Then don't stay up late playing your dumb video games on Saturday night!

I used to work nights and know the horrible feeling of *wanting* so badly not to be drowsy. I mean, good night... Bro. Sam Davison was my pastor! He's a master preacher! I hung on every word he said and would never want to miss a service because of his preaching! Yet even during *his* preaching I would get drowsy. I get it.

But if it's something you can help, do it. Go to bed earlier. Learn to drink coffee (takes a solid month to learn to like it black!) and use it as a tool to contribute to being timeless in the area of preaching. Pinch your leg. Bite your tongue. Take notes. Eat breakfast that morning. Do whatever it takes, but stay awake.

Stay Engaged. Being awake and being engaged are different. Your eyes can be open but your mind might be closed. Keep your mind on what is being said. Follow the preacher's thoughts. Keep up when he says, "Turn to..." Don't "snap out of it" when you hear everyone laughing at a joke you just missed. Don't let your eyes glaze over. Listen! Be engaged!

Sit up. Posture says a lot. When you are at church, do you slouch in your seat? If so, sit up. Guys, don't lean forward with your head down and stare at the floor. Sit up! Backs on the seat and eyes up. Contribute! Don't discourage.

Don't talk. Many youth ministries have a certain section of the church where the teens sit during the preaching. Don't do anything to distract others. Most importantly, don't talk. I love seeing you ignore your neighbor when he or she leans over to talk to you during the preaching. That's good. That's the only time you can be rude to your neighbor—when he or she is being rude to the preacher. Just straight up ignore him or her! Eyes forward, Bible open, straight face. Don't laugh, don't respond, and don't even flinch. Better yet, shout, "AMEN!" even if nothing amazing was just said. That'll scare them off!

Pre-read texts. If you are in a series and you know what text is coming up, read the text ahead of time. You will have questions come up in your mind and you will wonder what the preacher will say about this or that verse. You will have a grasp of where the preacher is coming from in the Scripture, and you will already be in the biblical author's flow of thought. You will understand the context better than anyone else, and you will be more excited about the preaching because you have invested in the service.

Change. Probably the most encouraging way to contribute to the timelessness of preaching is to make sure preaching works. How can YOU make sure preaching works? By changing.

Every week, something is preached from God's Word. If "All Scripture is given by inspiration of God, and is profitable," then that means every time you are confronted with the Bible there is something there for you. Apply it. Change. Let it work in you. Preaching is supernatural, but it won't override your will. You have to do your part to respond to the preaching. Let it change you.

Respect Is Given, Not Earned

As we were driving today, I saw a billboard for the Marines that said, "Earned, not given" with the Marine logo and a shiny silver cutlass underlining the motto. I understand the sentiment. I get it. Each Marine puts himself through grueling training in order to be shown respect, or else he would not deserve it.

On the other side of it, though, is the title of today's note: Respect is given, not earned.

Hm... That seems backwards, doesn't it? Don't we *earn* our respect? Don't we have to *work* for it?

Yep. You should work for others' respect. But... here's the catch... just because you've *earned* someone's respect doesn't mean they'll *give* you respect.

Do you think al-Qaeda respects our Marines? No. Of course not. *But how come?! They've EARNED their respect, haven't they?*

The Marines have done plenty to have earned respect, but respect is given, not earned. Just because someone earns your respect doesn't mean you have to GIVE them your respect. Right?

You choose whom to respect. You dole out respect to the people you want to respect. Sometimes, you choose to respect people whether they've earned it or not.

I respect President Obama, but, in my mind, he hasn't done anything to *earn* my respect. I have a skeptical view of most politicians and their goals and methods of taking power, so I don't even respect President Obama's journey to his presidency. All I respect about him is his office. I choose to show that respect, not because he's earned it, but because I give it.

So, choose to give respect out to people whether they have earned it or not. Tonight, you may or may not think Bro. Ruben has "earned" your respect. Maybe you don't know him, or maybe you hate his guts (yeah right!). Regardless of what you think of him, choose to show him respect by doing a few things:

1. **Quiet down.** When game time is over, please do not talk.

2. **Pay attention.** When it's preaching time, listen. Look up. Say "Amen." Get into his preaching.

3. **Thank him.** Afterwards, thank him for his work in

preparation, and for his time.

Have a great evening! I will see you next week!

"Is It Effective?"

Should our main question be, "Is it effective?"

Jesus was effective, but his opposition did not question His effectiveness. They questioned his *authority*. They knew that no matter how effective a minister might be, he only has a legitimate ministry when His authority comes from God. Jesus agreed.

I was listening to a podcast last week by someone I had never heard of. In training his church staff, a guiding question for them was, "Is it effective?" While I am not opposed to effectiveness, I think sometimes we let effectiveness trump legitimacy.

The point of this series is to encourage our church to stick to what we know is biblical lest we venture too far and end up with a ministry that is *effective* but lacks God's *power* [remember, *authority*, Mat. 28:18].

Last week, we covered several principles:

1. **God's authority is necessary to conduct legitimate ministry** (Jesus himself emphasized God's authority on his ministry).

2. **Jesus passed God's authority to the church** (not to individuals, but to the institution. "All *power* is given unto me... *Go ye*... unto the *end of the world*." Mat. 28:18-20)

3. **Churches pass that authority by planting other churches** (like Antioch laying hands on Paul and Barnabas as they went out to ordain elders in other cities, Acts 13:1-3).

Right doctrine = God's authority on a ministry.

We wouldn't accept a baptism from the Boy Scouts, would we?

Or the Salvation Army? Or a Catholic church?

No. We can show that their core doctrines do not line up with Scripture, so we cannot align our church with their doctrine by accepting their baptisms.

Tonight, let's talk about that a little more.

I Get Concerned For People Who Miss a Lot Of Church

This note was in preparation for revival services at our church...

I get concerned for people who miss a lot of church. I'm concerned for some of you.

Church needs to be a priority. Not for the CHURCH'S sake. For YOURS!

When I encourage you to be in church, it is not because I profit from it somehow. I get no bonuses from the corporate Baptist headquarters if I reach a certain number of people in our class (btw, there are no corporate Baptist headquarters.)

No. I encourage you to not miss church because I know it can help you.

Not because your friends are here. Not because it will make you rich. Not because we'll have a fun game on Wednesday. Nope.

I think you should come because men like Bro. Wilson are opening THE BIBLE and helping you be a less critical person (remember that lesson on Wednesday?) We're trying to help you with real-life issues, like when someone says, "Judge not!" and we're not sure what to say to that (again, from the lesson last Wednesday.)

Every service is a Bible service. Therefore, every service will help you.

Prayer times, Bible preaching, and even our game times—all of it is something God wants for your life.

I'm concerned when you miss church, because I'm afraid you are not committed to what's most important in life. I usually have no idea why you miss, but I think Mr. Sniffles attacks some manly men pretty hard. Ol' Mr. Sniffles and Ms. Sore Throat sure attack a lot of people. They're such cruel persecutors of the church.

Not only that, but I think the constant pressure of homework might be something the devil uses to distract you from what's most important in life—that which will benefit you in 264 years... your walk with God! I think homework is good to do. But NOT if you ignore God to do it. Seriously.

(On a side note, I think God gives you the ability to accomplish all he's called you to. If you are a full-time Master's student AND a church staff intern AND a new husband AND a thesis-writer all at once, GOD has to give the ability to get your homework and job responsibilities done... It just might take getting up at 3:30 daily to do it!)

I think church is SO important that you should commit to it. Like... seriously commit. I've seen people committed to band, football, baseball and boyfriends... what about church?

We have a revival service coming up in two weeks. Would you commit to being here every night of it? It will help you. It's God's Word being preached, and it's one of the finest men of God you'll EVER meet.

I hope you welcome Bro. Davison when he comes. I hope you come to church excited to hear from God. I hope you move closer to the front *(I was thinking about this... if a guest comes to our church and wants to find the BEST Christians—the ones who are CLOSEST to God and MOST excited about being right with him... where would they look for THOSE Christians? The front or back pew?)*

Remember when we talked about getting "into it?" Are you? Will you be? I'm not accusing. I'm just asking. And encouraging. It's best that way.

On Sunday, The Word Was Up In Your Business. How Rude.

This note came after a sermon from Isaiah 1 on the text "Wash you. Make you clean."

Sunday's sermon was about being clean vs. unclean. That makes some people nervous.

Sin makes us unclean. God can wash us clean.

Even after salvation, we sin. I don't know about you, but I feel dirty from my sin.

Did you ever go back and read Isaiah 1 after Sunday? It hurts to read it, because the preacher (Isaiah) *knows* how destructive sin is, and how much it will hurt the people he's preaching too.

Me too.

I hate when you know to do good, and do it not (James 4:17). It hurts me. My wife and I have long conversations about you—YOU—seriously... you, by name. If you're reading this, we talk about YOU and dream about how God will use YOU some day if you'll continue to serve him.

We fear the world's influence in ALL your lives—more so for some of you—and my first reaction is always to ask, "How can I preach the Word to help them avoid the pain that their sin will bring?"

My reaction is preaching. Mrs. Jamie's reaction is serving, texting, relating, loving, etc. Our reaction together, as a married unit, is to try to figure out how to help you.

We just started reading a Proverb a day as a family at breakfast. I love it. I forgot how GOOD Proverbs is. Man, it's packed with warnings!

I foresee some of you ignoring the warnings and getting hurt, and it hurts me to see that. No, I'm not Yoda—I can see the future a lot clearer than he can.

When the Word gets up in your business, challenging you to not just DO more, but to have a broken spirit and a contrite heart... listen to it. Obey the Word. Heed it. Hear it. Incline your ear to it. Bend your heart to God's will.

It's not rude, after all. In fact, it's love. Hm.

My Opinion – ALL Churches Should Have Clear Bible Teaching

Otherwise, why meet together?

To get entertained? The world does that better.

To teach you life skills? The world does that better.

To occupy some of your time? The world does that better.

If a church does not focus on clearly teaching the Bible, what's the point? That's one of the main purposes of church. The early church did it right in Acts 2:

And they continued stedfastly in the apostles' doctrine and fellowship, and in breaking of bread, and in prayers... And they, continuing daily with one accord in the temple, and breaking bread from house to house, did eat their meat with gladness and singleness of heart. Praising God, and having favour with all the people. And the Lord added to the church daily such as should be saved.

They focused on doctrine, fellowshipped together (hung out!) and praised God. In unity. They loved God, loved His Word (doctrine), and loved each other (fellowship). That's a healthy church that is others-focused.

So when we're ME-focused and inward-focused, we don't care about others. We don't care about doctrine. We don't care about praying.

Some churches lose the main emphasis of church, and think that the church's goal is to please everyone who comes, as if the church has this "All-new Gospel in shiny redesigned packaging" for sale.

Nothing's for sale here.

In fact, if you're saved, YOU have been bought, and you are not your own. Therefore, glorify GOD in your body, and in your spirit, which are God's. (1 Cor. 6) In my opinion, ALL churches should be places that remind people that God is the One to be pleased—not us.

Please HIM today.

Your Response Reveals Your Character

I preached a while back on Prov. 12:1 *"Whoso loveth instruction loveth knowledge: but he that hateth reproof is brutish."*

Our definition of a brute was "concretely stupid," or "dumb, set in concrete."

I was reading Proverbs 9 this morning at breakfast and these verses jumped out at me:

8 Reprove not a scorner, lest he hate thee: rebuke a wise man, and he will love thee. 9 Give instruction to a wise man, and he will be yet wiser: teach a just man, and he will increase in learning. 10 The fear of the Lord is the beginning of wisdom: and the knowledge of the holy is understanding. 12 If thou be wise, thou shalt be wise for thyself: but if thou scornest, thou alone shalt bear it.

Standing against God only hurts you, and fearing Him only helps you. Biblical reproof—when someone tries to help you from the Word—is only going to make you better.

Want to be better? Fear God, and love knowledge (sometimes it comes through correction.)

Want to be worse? Then ignore (or get mad at) reproof.

A parent, a pastor, a youth pastor, or ANYONE who tries to help you with Scriptural principles—even when they say stuff you don't like—is good for you.

What's your response when you're reproved. It says more about you then you realize. It tells you (and others) your character.

I've been encouraged by you—SEVERAL of you over the course of the last couple weeks and months—who have responded WELL when people have tried to help you. That says a lot about you, and I appreciate that. **I'm proud of you when you respond correctly**, because it takes a high level of maturity to respond well when you don't like the message. Good job.

Bible

If we emphasize anything in the Teens of Faith, it is that we are to love God and know Him through His Word. Spiritual depth can only come through Scripture, and once a teen learns to love the Bible, the rest of his spiritual life falls into place.

These are notes that emphasize the Bible in some way.

Where Are You In Your Bible Reading?

Where are you in your Bible reading?

That's a simple question I hope all of you can always answer. Not so you don't have to feel bad when you're asked... you should have an answer simply because you're in your Bible! That's a good reason.

I sure love our teens. I was with several other youth pastors last week, and I couldn't help but be thankful for where I am. I preached in a chapel this morning and couldn't wait to get to church with you. ☺ I want God's best for you and I pray for you often. Thank you for being a blessing.

So, beyond being a blessing to me personally, are you making that a long-term goal? Do you want to always be a blessing to others?

If yes, then learn the discipline of reading and loving your Bibles. Men, speak up when asked. Ladies, continue to have your sweet and meek spirits. Love God. Love others. Do right.

Is Bible Reading a Part Of Life

Is reading your Bible a part of life?

I was up in Big Bear this week for our staff planning, and every morning I walked out of our room to the living room where Bro. Si and Pastor were reading their Bibles. I'd join them and all morning we were just drinking coffee, enjoying the beautiful scenery and doing our devotions. I got through several chapters in Isaiah the last few days. It's a confusing book to read, but it's still helpful.

I don't know what Bro. Si or Pastor read the last couple of days. I don't know if it was life-changing. I don't know if they really remember everything they read. I don't know if they found the "Big Idea" while they were reading.

What I DO know is that they did their devotions. Also, I know they do them every day. And they've done them every day for years.

That takes discipline... but only for a while. The discipline is hard only at first, then it becomes a way of life. Is it that way for you yet? It doesn't take years or months... it only takes a few weeks for it to become a way of life—a habit.

I hope you do your devotions. Every now and then I'll ask some of you where you're at in your devos, and it's always a blessing to hear that you're doing them. You need to.

What would help you keep them going? A plan? Accountability? A booklet? I hope some day soon I can help with some of that... if you're interested. Devotions won't help you if you don't do them.

Work on disciplining yourself in the area of devotions.

Love the Bible

Do you love the Bible?

If so, you have a huge advantage over most Christians. Most Christians claim the name of Christ but don't care about His Word.

Did you wake up this morning focused on yourself or on the Bible? Were you excited to come to church to receive instruction, challenge and help from God's Word? Or were you mad at your sister, frustrated with your hair (Bro. Aaron?), distracted with homework, annoyed by your dog, rushed from waking up late or just generally tired from life?

What's your state of mind this morning? What do you have planned for tomorrow?

Make sure the Bible is part of your daily routine. I love you, and want God's best for you.

Giving, God's Word, and Grads Are Great

Today's the first day of our weekly offering in the Teens of Faith. Did you bring your dollar? Hopefully most of you received a letter in the mail this week about that, and a couple of you even texted me and said you're bringing yours today... Thank you for taking the time to communicate that! I appreciate it very much, and it's relieving and encouraging to see God working in your hearts!! If you missed last week or you want another one, feel free to grab a GIVE (sorry about the "FIVE" typo) booklet from off the table.

Also, if you missed on Wednesday, COME ON WEDNESDAYS! That was a subtle plug for Wednesday night attendance. We need you there for comedy night practice, but you need to be in church. On Wednesday we talked about memorizing Romans 8 this summer, and whether there's a prize or not, there should be something in each Christian that wants to know God's Word more and more and more and more and more and more. So grab a GOD'S GOD'S WORD booklet and be prepared to quote the first three verses by Wednesday. That's NOT too much to ask, in my opinion. You'd have a really hard time convincing me that that's too hard, too much, too soon, or too whatever. Don't make excuses, don't be lazy, and step up to the challenge. (*How inspirational, Bro. Ryan. Thanks.*) Sure, no prob.

C'mon... too chicken? Too scared? Can't do it? We'll see how many of you will!

On that note... Temecula kids... enjoy your first full week off and CONGRATULATIONS GRADUATES!! Woo hoo!! Do right (all of you, now). Love God. Love others.

In Busy Church Seasons, Don't Forget To Be a Christian

Never mistake church activity for spiritual growth. It's easy to get lost in all this big promotion and forget the big purpose of it all… that YOU live right… tomorrow!

We're not promoting big trips so that SOME DAY your life will be turned around by the preaching. We want you to go on these big trips with a heart that's ALREADY in tune with God and desiring to hear from Him. Big days can make you think, "Yeah. I did my spiritual thing this week. I'm right with God."

But,

- Did you read your Bible this week?

- Did you pray?

- Did you do right?

- Did you confess your sin and repent (turn away) from it this week?

- Did you purpose to come this morning and contribute to the services, or are you just here?

- By what you do today, will our church be able to "Rejoice evermore. Pray without ceasing. Despise not prophesyings."

- Are you rejoicing today?

- Are you eager about the preaching?

Don't mistake big days and events as your spirituality. Your personal walk with God is what makes you spiritual; not coming to a workday or going to our Preaching Rally. In all this big promotion for camp, the Heartland trip and the Preaching Rally, don't lose sight of the fact that the guy you'll sit next to in homeroom tomorrow is probably lost and could go to hell if he dies tomorrow night. Don't forget that your thoughts are being recorded by God, not just your actions. Don't forget to be... Christian. Do right, but love God first. The outward won't last if it doesn't come from the inward love for God.

Live In the Light

This note came after time change Sunday during our 1 Corinthians preaching series...

Has it been easier to wake up in the morning, now that it is light at 6:00 a.m.?

For me, if I see light outside, I feel like I'm missing out on something in life. This past week especially. I have had two big projects going on at church (which you'll see in a couple months), and every morning my eyes have just popped open at 4:30 or 5:00 a.m. It's still dark by then, but there's at least a glimmer of a sunrise way off in the distance. My coffee and the adrenaline of my projects help me wake up, but the time when my mind is really ready for the day is when the sun comes up. The daylight helps me really kick things into gear.

Daylight makes us come alive. It helps us think. It gives new life to every day. Imagine a place with no daylight—no fun! Boring! Lifeless.

But we get to live in sunlight... at least we get more than people in Alaska (in the winter, at least).

Do you live in the light every day? Spiritually speaking, now. Do you live in the light of God's Word? Does His truth shine on your life? Are you alive by Him? Can God shine a light on every part of your life and you not be ashamed? Does your life personify sincerity and truth?

Sincerity and truth (1 Cor. 5:8) are the hallmarks of living in the light. If God shines his spotlight on your life, would you be embarrassed or joyful? Live in the light.

"...to him it is sin."

James says, "Therefore to him that knoweth to do good, and doeth it not, to him it is sin." That's a rough verse, because we KNOW we should be doing a lot of stuff. But what about when we don't? Will God understand?

God knows we're human, but He also knows that we know to do right. How are you doing in some areas? Sinning? Or are you good?

Church Attendance. Are you missing church for homework or practices? Are you here every service you have a ride?

Prayer. Did you talk to the Father today? Are you planning on praying tomorrow? Did you pray throughout this whole week? If not, why not?

Giving. Are you obedient to the Bible when you are commanded to give? Are you tithing? If not, you are robbing God, according to Malachi. Are you giving to missions? Have is been a while since you gave in the TOF offering?

Bible Reading. Did you read your Bible this morning? Have you studied God's Word this week? Did you meditate on Scripture yesterday? Are you hearing from God daily?

You might KNOW you're supposed to do all these things, but are you doing them? If you know to do good, and you don't do it, "...to him it is sin."

There's Nothing More Encouraging Than YOU Doing These

There's Nothing More Encouraging Than YOU Doing These Things

You don't know what a blessing it is to hear about your spiritual growth week by week. I LOVED getting a couple encouraging "praying for you" texts last week, and it's awesome to see you having a good testimony on Facebook and with your friends. Try a few spiritual things to help you keep that up:

- Carry your Bible to school.

- Pass out one tract per day for the next month.

- Post an encouraging Bible verse every week.

- Come to EVERY service the next month. (AM, PM, Wed.)

- Dump ALL bad music and replace it with good stuff. (Even the one or two albums you really like!)

- Remove ALL bad movies you own.

- Ask your friends, "Hey, I'm trying to get better about my speech and my thoughts... would you not cuss around me any more?" And then hold them to it!

I've tried to say often that you're EXACTLY where you want to be spiritually. You're as eager to learn the Bible as you want, and those of you who REALLY have the zeal will push yourself to grow. You'll ask about books to buy, verses to memorize, and where to get tracts. You'll find ways to serve without being asked, you'll volunteer immediately for service, and you'll LOOK engaged in the services at church. (By the way, each of these things have been done by one or two people, but what about you?)

All I'm saying is, love God, love others, and choose to do right.

How Can We Deal With Depression

I taught a couple Bible classes at a local Christian school and included these notes...

In teaching at Linfield, we've come across several good topics that a lot of teens deal with. Our class discussions revolve around what the Bible has to say to our needs, and depression was one of the topics. It is interesting how prevalent depression is.

As Christians, our *first* response to depression should be belief in God. If you believe God is powerful enough to save you for eternity, it makes sense to believe that He is sufficient to meet your every need (read Colossians 1:9-22 for more on Christ's sufficiency), including any and all issues of depression.

The widespread issue of depression is often "answered" through drugs or drinking, or other ways of trying to retreat rather than conquer depression. Also, depression is treated as a disease—a chemical imbalance—far more often than a spiritual issue.

Although depression is caused from a variety of sources (biological factors, sense of disorder in life, parental issues, abuse, negative thinking, life stress, anger, guilt...), we must still ask the single question, "is Christ enough to meet every need?" If so, turn to Him (don't just *add* him to your pills) and be all-in.

Prayer is a simple way to "vent" to Someone who will hear you and be able to help you. The antidote to depression is to identify the source—the mind—and find out what the Bible has to say about the mind.

A perfect Bible passage is Philippians 4:8-9 "Finally, brethren, whatsoever things are **true**, whatsoever things are **honest**, whatsoever things are **just**, whatsoever things are **pure**, whatsoever things are **lovely**, whatsoever things are of **good report**; if there be any **virtue**, and if there be any **praise**, *think on these things*. Those things, which ye have both learned, and received, and heard, and seen in me, do: and the God of **peace** shall be with you."

Do you want peace instead of depression? Follow the Bible and flush your mind with the things in bold (truth, honesty, purity...). Paul told the Romans to be "transformed by the renewing of your mind" in order to be completely fulfilled in life. The right kind of transformation comes from the right kind of renewing of the mind. Renewal comes from truth, honesty, purity, etc.

The TOF class is all about teaching you how to mine out the

truth of God's Word in order to transform your life into the beauty it was designed to be.

Here are suggestions from Josh McDowell's *Handbook on Counseling Youth*. Purchase the book to find the full explanations of each point:

- Avoid being alone
- Seek help from others
- Sing
- Praise and give thanks
- Lean heavily on the power of God's Word
- Rest confidently in the presence of God's Spirit

Other Scriptures to read are: Genesis 15, 1 Kings 19, Psalm 119:25, Jonah 4, 2 Corinthians 4:1-18, Philippians 4:4-8, 1 Peter 5:7.

I love you, and want God to help you through your depression. Depression is big, but God is bigger. Let me know if you have any questions or comments.

Church, God, Jesus, EVERYTHING Sacred Is Pointless, Unless...

Without believing that the Bible is God's Word, everything we do related to God, the church, and our belief in these things is pointless. Right?

How do you know God? Well, we know the heavens declare the glory of God, and the firmament showeth his handiwork. We can spend time in nature looking at the intricacies of God's creation and marvel at His power. But we don't get to know God as our Saviour, Lord, Father and Friend through His creation.

We know Him through His Word.

We learn about His will for our lives through His Word.

We come to church because of His Word.

We preach, pray, sing, serve, and hire interns because of His Word (well, okay... maybe not the interns part).

God's Word is the only reason we meet weekly. On a Sunday. On your weekend!

Do you KNOW that the Bible you're holding is God's Word? Do you CARE? You should. It's the whole reason we do *anything* and *everything* related to church.

It is SO good for you to be able to KNOW that the Bible you hold really IS God's Word, and that you can trust it by faith. God said repeatedly that He wants you to know His truth. And He's given it to us.

Do you CARE? Show it by getting into God's Word.

BIBS

BIBS (Big Idea Bible Study) is one of the only preaching series we have ever repeated in the Teens of Faith. We learned about HOW to study the Bible, and then practiced it through weekly discussions related to the teens' daily *BIBS Devotional*.

These announcement sheets cover several years' worth of BIBS lessons.

Books To Help You

Tools are used in every profession, and good money is spent to increase learning and effectiveness. You as a Christian should have tools to help your Christian life, and the Christian's tools are... books. Here are a few books that I'd encourage you to spend about $40 or $50 on (see gettextbooks.com for cheap prices listed):

- *The King James Bible Commentary*; Nelson Publishers; contributions by Dobson, Feinberg and more. About $14

- *A Survey of the Old Testament*; by Hill and Walton; Zondervan (2nd edition is cheaper) About $10

- *Jensen's Survey of the New Testament*; Moody Press. About $17

- *World's Bible Handbook*; Boyd. About $13

Not everyone will buy these, but if you're serious about God and finding out His direction for your life, you'll be serious about finding answers in God's Word. If you're digging for direction (and you should be) you should have a hunger to know what God says, and these books can help you. It's just a thought.

Gru asks the Bible, "Why are you so OLD?"

The wise Gru says, "Why are you so OLD?"

Have you ever wondered that about the Bible? It's okay if you have... I have!

God, what good is the Bible today? It's so OLD! It doesn't make sense! I'm confused.

You're not a terrible person if you don't understand the Bible... you're normal. It was written in a whole different language! It was written to people WAY different from us. It was written to people with WAY different problems than we have.

No. Scratch that last sentence. Because the problems THEY faced in the Bible are the same problems WE face today. They didn't have the drug problems in their public schools, they didn't have the media distracting people from their life's purpose, they didn't have the internet at their fingertips on their cell phones... but they did face sin, and God did provide a way out: salvation.

The Bible TRUTH is the same yesterday, today, and forever, because Jesus is the same. The APPLICATION might be different today, but the TRUTH is the same, and it will never change.

If you can learn to grow yourself through God's Word, that removes a lot of the need for the ups and downs of the Christian life.

Do right. Love God. Love others. We love you!

This Is the Best Way I Know To Influence You Toward God:

This note came midway through our BIBS Bible study series...

Whether you're "getting it" or not, I have to believe that this series has been a help to you. If I thought I was wasting my time I'd change series immediately, but I don't know if there's a better subject you could be learning than... the Bible.

I love you all very much and I'm passionate about your spiritual growth. The best way that I know to influence you toward Christ is not to motivate you, intimidate you or try to get you to do what I say (all those methods fail over time); the best thing you can catch from me is a passion for God's Word.

Nothing else will matter in life. Sure, you might "make it" in life and be successful, but you won't be satisfied outside of knowing God through His Word. Nothing is sweeter than a relationship with God. Abundance. Fellowship. It's awesome!

Anyway, I hope you want it for you as much as I want it for you.

Love God. Love others. Do right.

Even Habakkuk Is Interesting When You Understand It

This note came after our class studied Habakkuk...

Wasn't last Wednesday cool?

Who knew that Habakkuk had anything to say to us? Well... apparently YOU knew, because you were the ones who dug it all out, right from the Bible! I felt like I was in a roomful of scholars; it was great to see you getting it.

Nothing is more rewarding for a preacher than to be understood. The spiritual growth all comes from God, but the human aspect of preaching and teaching requires study, presentation AND listeners. When the Bible gets all the way to where the listeners understand it, the human aspect is over and the Spirit goes to work on man's spirit to convict, encourage, challenge, comfort, etc. My joy in working with you is when you move from hearing to doing.

Do right!

How'd Your First Week of BIBS Go?

This note came after our teens started our BIBS Devotionals, available at CalvaryBaptist.pub...

As you know, last week we gave you the BIBS devotional and you started on them Thursday.

How'd it go?

Did you get something on paper every day? I'm not asking you if you filled out all the days on the trip to church tonight to make it look like you filled it out every day. I'm asking if you were dedicated to your devotions this week.

Hopefully BIBS becomes a habit. All of you have the time... it's how you use your time that makes the difference. Some of you spend a lot of time on Facebook, on homework, on computer reboots... what about your devotions? How'd that go this week?

BIBS isn't something you're doing so you can go on a missions trip. BIBS is something you should do to help your spiritual life. Get in the Bible. Love your Bible. Read your Bible. Think about your Bible. Know your Bible. Live your Bible.

Today was an application day in the BIBS format, so hopefully this week has shown you some ways that you can grow in the Lord. Have you done anything different based on your study of God's Word? If you were challenged from your Bible and you haven't made any changes yet, make some changes! No one likes to be deceived... but God says "But be ye doers of the Word and not hearers only, deceiving your own selves."

Warning: Weekly BIBS Checks Might Get Awkward

Our midweek services were gender-separated class discussions relating to the daily BIBS devotions that the students did...

In the split sessions, I'm going to be asking direct questions to basically each of you guys. "Why didn't you do it this week?" That's pretty direct!

The Christian life is about growing spiritually, and I have NO problem helping you in your Bible reading by making things uncomfortable for you.

Laziness is no excuse. Time is no excuse. There's almost NO excuse. Ok let's put it this way, there will be NO excuse before God, right? So would I be a good youth pastor if I ever said, "It's okay to not read your Bible." NO!

I believe I'll give account to God for my work as a youth pastor in training and helping you grow spiritually. If that means that I or my wife or the Bakers have to confront you about something then so be it. We try to spend a lot of time encouraging, teaching and helping you... but there may need to be some rebuke, confrontation and challenge in there as well.

Can you take it? I think you can.

It's all for your spiritual benefit. I don't know how else to tell you except that I love you all and want God's best for you, and you'll never have God's best outside of a personal relationship with Him.

Love God. Love others. Do right.

Are You As Good As a Disneyland Employee?

Periodically you're asked to do stuff.

And you're always willing to do it. Praise God! Thank you for your servant's spirit. It's refreshing to be around people who love to serve.

My wife and I watched a documentary on Disney parks and one of the standout features is their passion for serving. It seems like every worker is all about helping people. It seems like everyone there is happy. We LOVE to be around people who love to serve us. So when YOU are that kind of servant, you are a testimony to others everywhere!

Hopefully you have been challenged from your *BIBS* Devotions to have a faith that is REAL (like the Thessalonians had). Your faith should not just be something that you believe, but it should change your day-to-day lives. Your Christianity should be something that causes you to sacrifice (ch. 2), to endure any type of persecution (ch. 2), to constantly mature (ch. 3), and to be pure (ch. 4). If your faith is real, it will show up LOTS of different ways in your life (ch. 5)!

So thank you for letting it show up. You're a blessing to be around. Keep doing right. Keep loving God. Keep loving others. We love you!

Don't Take a Christmas Break From Your Walk With God

This note came over Christmas break...

Enjoying your break from school?

Don't take a break from the Lord! BIBS is a daily devotion, including on Christmas Day—and all the other days of your vacation. After all, we're always saying "Jesus is the reason for the season." Is that just a catch phrase we throw around? Or is that real to us? Is it real to you? Hopefully. Jesus should be bigger to you than anything else this season, and I pray you give Him His due honor and respect by listening to Him through His Word.

Daily devotions is a discipline that I hope all of you get in the habit of doing. It is not something that will magically transform you into super-Christian, but it will help you and gradually grow you over time. Get in God's Word, and live God's Word.

Nothing else matters. Your side jobs, your school, your family, your fun—all these take second place to the Lord. They should, anyway!

I sure love all of you and I hope you know that everything we do and say as the youth staff is meant to be a help to you. Being in your Bible is not for Bro. Ryan's benefit but for yours, even if you do not see it that way yet. Love God more than anything else in life and watch Him transform your future.

Love God By Loving His Word

The preacher challenged us, "Read your Bible for at least 5 minutes, every day."

"I can do that," I thought. "5 minutes is easy enough."

In junior high at summer camp I decided to make Bible reading a priority. I got home from camp on Saturday, crashed on the couch for a couple hours, woke up, had dinner with my family and went right back to bed.

Until Sunday morning.

Just a few days before, I had decided to read my Bible more. At the Friday night campfire I had given a testimony in front of all those people that I was going to read my Bible more.

But that Sunday morning, I forgot. Sunday mornings never really started with Bible reading, so it never crossed my mind.

Remembering. The first hurdle I had to overcome in my Bible reading was actually remembering to do it! I knew I should— God had convicted me through the preaching—but it was hard to actually do. I had to, you know, work at it. I had to... try.

Too bad. So sad. I thought this "5 minutes a day" thing was going to be a breeze, but I failed my first day!

Have you ever been there? Can you relate?

I know a lot of people who know that they should read their

Bible. I've even heard testimonies from people, like me, who committed to reading their Bible more. In front of everyone they said, "God, I commit to read my Bible at least _____ minutes per day."

I have seen those people fail. Yep, just like me.

It's hard! I get it! Just remembering to read every day is hard. Even if you make a commitment to God—it's still hard!

Understanding. As if remembering to read isn't hard enough, we also need to get it when we read. Or else the reading is pointless.

Granted, there's a certain level of blessing that comes from just the discipline of reading your Bible every day, but the real blessing is in the content of what is there.

You Have To Get It — the Bible, I Mean

It seems like it should go without saying, but just reading your Bible isn't the real goal. You should understand what you're reading.

For me, getting into the habit of reading my Bible began with a one-year Bible. I would read my section each day as faithfully as I could. When I would miss a day, I would work to catch up, but if I got too far behind, it seemed hopeless! There were too many pages to read!

Then, when I would get all inspired to "catch up," I would end up speed-reading (read this as "skimming.") The problem was, I didn't understand any of it.

Even when I was reading faithfully each day and rarely missing a day (into my high school years), I still would not fully understand what I was reading. I would read, yes, but it only helped me a little.

I would catch a verse here or there that was a blessing, or I would see an old sermon note that would provide an outline of what I was reading. But I could never really step back and see the big picture. I never saw the Bible as a book... I always saw it as a collection of verses.

I read other books all through high school, just for fun. I read several Frank Peretti books, the Indian in the Cupboard series, a few of the Horatio Hornblower series, some Nancy Drew and Hardy Boys mysteries, all of Bro. Ed Dunlop's books and more.

When I read novels, I knew what I was reading. I would start at the beginning, follow the author's storyline as the plot unfolded, and reach the story's climax with the author. I would conclude each chapter or section understanding what the author was saying.

When I read my Bible, though, I treated it like a different kind of book. Instead of looking at it like a novel where the author has a flow of thought, I treated it like I had always treated the Bible: I opened it to a verse and just started reading.

Do you ever do that with a novel? What novel do you open up to page 72 and just start reading in the middle of a paragraph?

Hopefully, BIBS gives you a little bit of structure to your daily reading. We want to start with Observation (birds-eye view), then move to Interpretation (understanding the text), and then Application (what's it mean to me?)

Pay attention tonight to try to get into the author's flow of thought.

4 Tips For Establishing Morning Devotions

Do you spend time each morning doing personal devotions?

Personal devotions are simply a time that you set aside every morning to read God's Word, think about it, and pray to God. It is not the *only* time to have a relationship with God (that goes on all day every day), but your morning devotional time is crucial to a solid walk with God. You will be very distant from God without spending time with Him in His Word.

A few simple suggestions on daily devotions:

- **Make time daily.** Set your alarm and make it part of your morning routine. Be committed to it. If you do it as your *duty* for a while, eventually it becomes *routine,* and then it becomes something you *enjoy*, and then it becomes something you *can't miss.*

- **Listen.** Audio Bibles are everywhere, and you can download a million Bible apps that include the audio version. I use the YouVersion Bible app and sometimes listen to the King James Bible audio version. Instead of listening to music while you jog, work out, or drive to school, try listening to your Bible instead.

- **Get a schedule.** That same app also has daily Bible reading schedules. Some are long, some are short. Get yourself on a schedule and keep to it every day. Some schedules are daily, while others might do 6 days per week.

- **Make a prayer list.** Get a journal, an Evernote notebook, or a Microsoft Word document and write down things to pray for. Then, each day, open up your journal and talk to God about the things on your list. Your list might include praises, prayer requests, struggles you're having, relationships, life questions, etc.

Do you spend time each morning doing personal devotions? If not, what about starting tomorrow?

Daily Devotions Are... Daily

This note came midway through our weekly BIBS Devotional class discussions...

Do you do daily devotions?

Not weekly. Not monthly. Not never-ly. Daily?

That's a HUGE discipline to master. If you can get disciplined about daily devotions, you'll be ahead of most of the world— including many Christians! I'm encouraged to see on my Bible app how many people completed various Bible reading plans this year. It's good to know that there are lots of Christians reading God's Word.

Someone said, "The person who DOESN'T read is no better off than the person who CAN'T read."

There are people in your life—present AND future—who *need* you to read. They will be counting on you to become a reader as you lead and help others. If you read nothing else... read your Bible.

How's it been going? Have you missed a day or two? That's okay! Just pick it back up this afternoon!

Let me be ultra-super-clear. Bible reading is NOT a shame thing. It is NOT a competition. It is NOT a test. There are NOT right or wrong answers, so you won't be able to look better or worse than others. Shame and "testing" turns into lying and cheating... this is your BIBLE we are talking about!

Being accountable in your devotions is about encouraging Christians to get in God's Word. That's it. It takes SLOW people about 20 minutes to do. For an average reader, we're talking about 15 minutes of reading.

For your own sake, and the sake of others who count on you being a REAL Christian—inside and out—develop the habit of daily devotions. If you can do that, you're on the path of God's promised blessing of abundant Christian living (John 15).

Summer Days Shouldn't Start Without Being In the Word

This note came several months after we completed our BIBS series...

Many of you were so faithful to be in your Bible every day, and it showed.

Has that slipped? Have you been as faithful to your devotions as GOD would want you to be? Not me! I know I can do better, and I am sure you can, too.

This summer, make it a new-summer's-resolution to never miss one day of devotions. I like what Keli said in her testimony on Sunday—that she doesn't like to start her day not *without* getting in the Word.

I hope that's true of all of us.

And guess what, if you miss a day (or, should I say *when* you miss?), that's okay... read tomorrow. I'm serious.

If you miss a WEEK, that's okay... read tomorrow.

If you've NEVER read your Bible, that's okay... read tomorrow!

Don't beat yourself up for what you're NOT doing. Just start doing what you know is right!

Being at church isn't enough. Not cussing isn't enough. Coming to camp isn't enough. Loving God isn't enough. It HAS to show in what comes OUT of your life. Bible reading, Bible meditation, Bible study, a prayer time—these are all evidences of REAL love of God.

Are you real?

Let this summer show it in your personal morning routine. I have BIBS books available if you want to have an outline. Otherwise, start. Start tomorrow!

Summer Devotions – Think and Meditate

This note came the following week...

Last Wednesday I wrote about your summer devotions.

Since then, how many days have you read your Bible?

Did you read anything on Thursday? How about Friday? How about Saturday before Saturation?

Your morning devotional time doesn't have to be a crazy 3-hour summit every day. Read. Meditate. Pray. Sometimes in that order. Sometimes not.

Reading is often emphasized when we're talking about devotions, and prayer is often mentioned, too. But what about meditation?

Meditation is the simplest of all of them, I think. All you have to do is stop and think. I like meditation the most because I get to use my *imagination*. Don't just *read*, but *meditate*.

Stop and think a while about what you're reading.

Are you in the Old Testament? Meditate on whatever story you're reading. Pastor's been preaching about the tabernacle. Hasn't that been cool? He's painted the picture of the badger-skin walls, the silver pedestals, and the wash basin and what it took to carry those things through the desert. If you're reading a story, *meditate* on it and sit there beside David in the cave, feeling what he's feeling as he writes a Psalm.

Are you in the New Testament? Imagine yourself as a church member in Ephesus, and Paul's writing to *your church* specifically! How cool is that?! *Meditate*—take time to stop and think—about what's being said to you.

Sometimes preaching is just teaching you how to meditate. Preaching—like this morning—is taking simple words (just one verse again) and making it come alive.

Do you meditate on Scripture? Try it tomorrow!

Bible Study Is Easy When You Break It Down

This note came in the middle of a busy season in our youth ministry…

Memorizing Comedy Night skits is good.

Meditating on Scripture is best.

Remember Sunday school? We easily spent a half-hour together just thinking—looking at words and thinking about them.

How easy was that, right?

- **The way** – path. Lots of people walking down the path. Choices. Fork in the road.

- **Fool** – I don't want that to be me! Someone devoid of wisdom.

- **Right** – righteous. "I'm good."

- **His own eyes** – only he thinks he's good. God doesn't.

- **But** – praise God for that! We don't have to be fools!

- **He that** – ME! And YOU! Praise God!

- **Hearkeneth** – listens intently and intentionally. Perks his ears up.

- **Counsel** – the greatest Counsellor is Jesus Christ (Isaiah 9:6). Psalm 119:24 Thy testimonies also are my delight and my <u>counselors</u>.

- **Wise** – makes sense. I want to be that.

Studying Scripture is fairly easy. You just have to think. Think about each word. It's amazing what pops out to you when you meditate on Scripture.

So how'd it go this week?

Did you wake up Monday and get in the Word?

Think about it right now. Stop reading and think. Stop reading! Come on... stop reading and think about Monday!

Now what about Tuesday?

How about this morning?

It's GOOD if you read the Bible. It's GOOD if you meditated on your Comedy Night skit lines.

It's BEST if you meditated on Scripture.

BIBS Is Restarting Soon — From Past To

Future

This note was in preparation for a re-launch of the BIBS Series...

Many of you were too young to be involved in the Alaska Missions Trip and the preparation that went into that. For months ahead of our trip we planned and prepared.

We announced the trip in the Fall and worked all Winter and Spring on BIBS, the Big Idea Bible Study method and devotionals. Remember that series?

After preaching on Wednesday nights about WHY and HOW to study your Bible, we actually started doing it. Each week you were given a passage to read and think about. Then, you would write in your BIBS devotional what God spoke to you about through His Word. Finally, we would meet on Wednesdays and discuss 1) What God said in the text and then 2) What God said *to you* through the text.

It was the most spiritual growth I'd ever seen in a group in such a short amount of time. I praised God for the growth He brought to you in those months.

Have you noticed something so far in this note? So far it has been in the past tense.

Forget past tense.

Let's move ahead. Let's look forward.

Instead of all the cool things happening to the Teens of Faith from 3 years ago, let's think about the Teens of Faith of next summer!

Like... you! Think of where you'll be in a year. Another school year gone, and another summer ahead. Seems crazy to think about, right?

Well, where will you be, spiritually? I said on Wednesday that if you have ever been closer to God than you are now, then right now you are backslidden.

Draw nigh to God through His Word. Learn how to do it through BIBS. Starting in 2 weeks on Wednesdays. Can't wait...

"I'm Into God, Just Not the Bible."

I have heard people say something to this effect: "I'm into God; I'm just not into reading the Bible."

I cannot be critical. I have been there, too. Haven't you?

I can understand when someone says that they are not "into" the Bible. I have been there. I have found it sometimes confusing, frustrating, or (I'll just say it...) boring. Am I alone in this? I think not.

Regardless of what I feel about the Bible, though, God has a clearly different opinion. It is, in fact, impossible to separate God from the Bible. In that sense, John 1:1 clears up a lot of confusion for us: "In the beginning was the Word, and the Word was with God, and the Word was God."

Jesus Christ is God is the Bible is God's Word.

Someone who loves someone else will be interested in deepening their relationship through communication. I love my wife and have letters from her in my wallet, in my dresser, in my drawers, in my suit coat pockets and on my office walls. I am interested in what she has to say, because I'm "into" her. I love her.

Someone who is "into" God MUST also be into His Word. God's Word is how we can know Him.

So are you "into" God, really? Here's your test:

1. How much do you *care about* His Words to you?

2. How much do you *ingest* His Words (reading, sermons, etc.)?

3. How much do you try to *live* His Words?

It is a tough test, but one we must all take from time to time.

This BIBS series cannot make you care about God's Word. It

will not make you read more or faster. It will not change how you live. YOU have to do all those things.

What this series WILL do is hopefully inspire you to *want* to know God more through His Word, and then give you the tools to know how to do that better.

I love the Bible. I love God and I want to know Him better. For about 15 years now, I have tried to do that almost every day, personally. It has been the best 15 years of my life, for sure!

Get "into" God my getting into His Word.

Definition: The Bible is the Word of God, progressively penned by Divinely inspired humans to eternally convey God's thoughts to man.

How Have You Done This Month?

You can know all about Bible study, but have you studied your Bible this month? I am not accusing; I am just asking.

It is easy to fall into the devil's trap of knowing *about* God but not really *knowing* God. We can know a lot *about* His Word by reflecting on our kids' Bible storybooks. *Sure,* you think, *I know about Daniel, Joseph, David, Paul and Peter. I know a LOT of Bible.*

But what is the point of those Bible stories? Do you know that? Do you know what God *said* and what God is *still saying* through the story of David and Goliath? Have you learned to trust God in the face of obviously impossible odds? Have you continued to stand for truth despite the consequences, like Daniel?

What have you read this month? First of all, have you understood it? Second, have you done anything different because of it?

Bible stories are mere stories—no different from other historical stories—if the necessary step of Application is not done.

Again, how have you done this month? Have you been reading the Scriptures more fervently and faithfully than ever before? Have you worked harder to understand them? Have you been more diligent to study?

BIBS Accountability Will BE a Help To You

BIBS is about Bible study, but NOT for the sake of you preaching, giving a devotion, or impressing people with your Bible knowledge. BIBS is about Bible study for the purpose of *life change*. You'll never be close to God without drawing nearer to Him through His Word. It's impossible! So, BIBS is about helping you draw close to God, for the sake of drawing close to God.

Your personal devotions are personal, but accountability will help you grow personally. We have a lot of fun together at activities, but what about being Scripturally relevant with each other, and edifying each other? You know... like the Bible says we should do. What about helping the weaker brethren, and encouraging each other to do right.

Godly peer pressure is an awesome thing.

So, dive all in.

I Am Excited For Wednesday

This note helped prepare our students for the BIBS discussion times.

This Wednesday will be our first "official" time gathering together to discuss our BIBS Devotions that we've been doing each day. We'll start class with our little game, have some announcements, and then split into separate classes.

This is NOT about getting the "right answer." We are discussing what God has spoken to YOU about. This is not an exact science. The goal is not to be seen by others... the goal is that you grow in God!

Lying is pointless. Lying about doing your devotions is kind of… silly! You're actually a MORE honest person, and BETTER off as a Christian when you're able to humble yourself and admit that you're not perfect, or that you missed a few days (or ALL days) of devotions.

Get back on track. If you've missed a few days (like, you've been busy with family and Christmas break and…), then get back on track today. You don't have to redo everything you've missed (unless you want to). The **best way to catch up is to start on TODAY'S devo,** then go back and fill in past days whenever you have time.

"Bro. Ryan… I don't know how to do it!" That's okay! Join the club! There are LOTS of us who don't know how to do it. The good news is, we're all in this together, and there's no "right" answer. It's about what you got from reading your Bible last week. That's all. Even if what you got was "I want to be a wise person," that's GOOD!

Be accepting and loving. This isn't some touchy-feely weird thing to say… it's Bible. Loving God and loving others is about doing everything in your power to bring others to the same relationship you have with God. If your goal is that others know God better, you will be encouraging rather than self-conscious. You will be humble rather than arrogant. You will think the best of others and be helpful, honest, and open. Sometimes, admitting that YOU don't know how to do it is all some people need to hear to be encouraged.

Don't snicker or belittle. When people are brave enough to speak up in class, let's make sure to never laugh or belittle them for their answers. It's a BIG deal for introverts to speak up in class. One way to hurt people is to make their viewpoint seem dumb (by laughing or scoffing *psh). Avoid this, *please*!

I love you all. I want this to be helpful to you.

Our First Discussion Time Is Tonight

This note helped prepare the teens for BIBS discussions...

Tonight, we start our split discussions. We'll start class with a nice little game, have a few announcements, and then the ladies will dismiss to the Merry Hearts room for our first split session.

Here are a few things to keep in mind tonight:

Be involved. Don't leave the talking to the talkative people—you know... those loud-mouths that dominate every group conversation like Skye, Kaite, or Matthew (just kidding!). YOU speak up. We'll try to get answers from everyone.

It's okay if you missed some. I get it... last week was Christmas, and you might have slacked a little on a couple days here and there. Am I right? That's okay. I did a little "pencil pushing" myself (when you go back to previous days and fill in the blanks just so it doesn't look empty.) I do my BIBS at church, when I'm here, but I do the devotional part at home. I just had to fill in the blanks once I got to work, and because we had time off for Christmas, I filled in a few days at a time.

Be honest. You don't have to lie. That makes things *worse!* No one (including you) is better off if you lie about doing your BIBS, so just be honest. Who knows... maybe someone will be encouraged to know they aren't the *only* ones who struggled with this last week. I'm thinking, since this was our first week, we ALL struggled with this, and no one wants to admit it first! That's OKAY! That's GOOD, actually! Just be honest.

Think along with the group. Even if you weren't able to do each day's study, at least keep your mind open tonight. Think along. As we read each passage, stay engaged. Listen. If a thought comes to you, speak up. You might think, "I shouldn't speak up. I didn't even DO the work at home!" That's okay. If you have something to say, say it.

All answers are valid. I might have written down something *completely* different from you. Or... we might have basically the same thing. So what? It's not about what *I* wrote down... it's about what YOU wrote! So remember... this is ALL about you spending time with God. Who am I to tell you what's "right" or "wrong" about that? Everything God spoke to you about is valid. Share it tonight without fear.

Suspend judgment. Meaning... don't judge others' answers. If someone who's younger than you says something you think is dumb, don't show it. In fact... change how you think about it. Encourage them.

Come with a "that was good" attitude. Turn your thoughts from negative to positive. Instead of thinking everyone else's answers are dumb, or everyone else is trying to kiss up to the teacher... forget those mean or selfish thoughts and instead think kind thoughts of others. No matter who it is, decide NOW to get something from tonight. "Wow. That was a good answer... I never thought of that... I didn't even see that... Oo, that was cool that he said that... Nice insight..." It all starts with your attitude. So work on your attitude now, before we begin.

Learn as you go. You might be showing up tonight thinking, "I had NO idea what I was doing!" That's okay. That's the same with a lot of us. We are learning as we go. That's why we're here at church, right? To learn? To grow? To become better? Otherwise (like, if you had this all down already), what's the point? You've already "arrived" (uh oh... now we're talking about the pride aspect from last week's SS sermon). Come to learn. If you have completely different answers, share them, too!

I promise I will do my best to not make you feel dumb for anything you say. Can you promise that, too?

My BIBS Big Ideas For Several Proverbs Passages

This note came after a few weeks of BIBS discussions...

We discussed these passages in class. If you were wondering about how we arrived at some of our answers, here is my 2 cents' worth. There are no "right" answers. These are just mine:

These loosely follow the word, phrase, sentence, question, answer, combine steps.

Prov. 1:1-6

- Wisdom
- Gaining wisdom
- A wise man will gain more wisdom
- what happens when we gain wisdom?
  - understand wisdom
  - increase learning
  - gain knowledge and disc.
  - gets counsel
- **God gives us all kinds of blessings when we search for His wisdom.**

1:7-19

- Wicked
- Wicked people
- Wise people should avoid the wicked
- Why should...
  - v9 ornaments
  - 10-commanded
  - 11-12 do BAD things
  - 13-greedy
  - 16-violent
  - 19 - *takes* life, doesn't give it
- **Since there's so much bad associated with the wicked, we should fear God and seek wisdom**

instead.

- (bad influences can include friends, online, books, articles, movies... Who are we listening to?)

1:20-33

- wisdom
- wisdom cries
- wisdom cries for us to follow her
- Why does wisdom...
  - she wants us to
  - too many people ignore her
  - she's best
  - there's bad associated with ignoring her
  - 33 safety in wisdom, no fear of evil
- **If we want to avoid all the bad from ignoring wisdom, we should follow after her.**

2:1-9

- searching
- searching for wisdom
- we should diligently search for wisdom
- why should we diligently...
  - v9 understand righteousness, judgment, equity, good path
- **Because wisdom pays off in righteousness, judgment, equity, good path, I should <u>diligently</u> do my part to seek it.**
  - (diligence of daily devotions, MY job, MY

responsibility, personal relationship with God, takes discipline, setting alarm, waking up, not passively expecting wisdom to come to me)

2:10-22

- Deliverance
- wisdom delivers
- wisdom delivers from various evils.
- HOW does wisdom deliver us? or WHAT does wisdom deliver us from?
  - evil man 12-15
  - it preserves us 10
  - evil woman 16-19
  - sets us on good path 20-21
  - avoids death-22
- **Wisdom delivers us from evil men and women, and guides us in right ways.**

Do Your BIBS, But Do Them With the Right Heart

God would rather have your heart than your sacrifice. He thoughts so way back in the Old Testament, and He still thinks that today.

Israel got good at getting the right answer. The Pharisees had ALL the "right" answers.

But they missed the point of who God was and what He wanted. He did not want strict obedience. God wanted (and wants) His people to love Him and know Him.

We can do that today through His Word. Our weekly BIBS

discussions, and your daily devotions, are not about getting the "right" answer. There's not really a right answer. There's more like... a HEART behind what you do.

"Heartless" devotions looks like:

- I forgot to do it.

- I'm going to fill out the form and SAY that I did 5 days, so it looks like I'm being honest and missed 2 days, but I really missed 3 or 4.

- I'm not going to think too hard about which day I missed. I'll just fill this form out.

- OOPS! It's Wednesday!! I'd better fill some things out in my book so it looks like I did my BIBS!

- Psh. Who cares? We'll just talk about it on Wednesday anyway. Big deal if I miss.

- I STARTED out strong, but now I'm "over" the excitement. Now it's boring. Now I don't even do them any more.

This list could go on. But what SHOULD it look like? Many of you have the right attitude about your BIBS, which looks like this:

- I love what I'm doing.

- I'm tired, but I NEED this.

- I've committed, so I'm going to do this every day.

- OOPS! It's Wednesday! Well... I missed this WHOLE week... but I'm not going to lie on my sheet.

- God, I love you. SO much. I want to know you. I want to walk wisely. Can you help me with that today.

- [next day] God, I love you. SO much. I want to know you. I want to walk wisely. Can you help me with that today.

- I'm not sure if anyone else will write this, but THIS is GOOD! I'm SO excited about what God showed me in

His Word!

- My Bible—I'll admit—is confusing sometimes, but it's getting easier, and I'm enjoying it more.

That type of spirit is MUCH sweeter.

Don't lie on your sheets. Don't do your BIBS just to go on the missions trip for free. Don't be a Pharisee. Love God. Love others. Do right.

Take It From a Lady Who's Read Her Bible 30+ Times!

This note came after a 6-week break from class accountability...

Prov. 24:10 says, "If thou faint in the day of adversity, thy strength is small." We should do right when it's *easy* AND when it's *hard*.

Sometimes when we think of Scripture, we go to the "usual" applications. i.e. "A husband who goes through hard times will walk out on his commitment to marriage."

Okay. But none of the teen guys are married.

Where can YOU be committed? Where have YOU failed when the work gets hard?

Let's get real... How about your daily devotions?

In tracking our accountability, when we got back to our weekly meetings together (after 6 weeks off class), your numbers picked back up!

One of the most important life principles is that you—YOU—should have a relationship with God. A personal walk with Him. It has to be real. He speaks through His Word, and it's the main way to hear His voice. A good relationship with God is *impossible* without a consistent diet of God's voice.

I like Mrs. Wilson's testimony from last week. She told the

ladies that when she was newly saved, someone told her that she should read the Bible through each year, and Mrs. Wilson was just crazy enough to believe it would help her! So she has... thirty-something times!

That's pretty cool. Adversity has come to her, I'm sure, but she hasn't fainted yet! I'd say her strength is pretty not-small.

Practical

These notes give some simple steps to act on the principles of Scripture...

Principles and the Practical

The **principle** is the reason behind what we believe and do. The **practical** is what we do. The practical is *what*; the principle is *why*.

We should have reasons for believing the way we believe, and doing what we do. Our church is built on biblical principles, and we are the way we are because we believe that is how the Bible is guiding us to be.

Benjamin Franklin—a man who thought logically and critically about life—was turned off by a church that said they had certain beliefs, but never made it clear that those beliefs came from God. To Mr. Franklin, religion seemed man-made, and he felt every bit as qualified to contrive his own virtues as well as the next man or church.

As Christians, we should be people who not only do *what* is right, but we should also know *why*, too. So, we have principles that guide us and practical steps to show us what to do.

The principles of Bible study are simple. We start with a preconception (based on faith, logic and evidence) that the Bible is supernaturally preserved as God's Word to us. We study it with basic principles—the first of which we will look at tonight: Observation.

The practical real-life examples that we will discuss tonight are not exhaustive, but they will serve as simple guides to help you read and understand the Bible.

If you can learn to take the *principles* of Scripture and translate them into *practical* changes you can make in your daily life (and DO them!), you will be right where God wants you to be, spiritually.

You want to be in God's will? Do you want to know His wisdom for you tomorrow? Do you want to make wise choices this week?

Start tomorrow by reading your Bible. Ask yourself, "So how is THIS Scripture I'm reading today profitable? What is the principle (what God *said*), and how does this principle affect me (what God is *saying*)?

You're Best When

1. You're real. There's nothing cool about faking anything. Everyone sees through you.

2. You serve. The disciples asked Jesus, "Who's going to sit by your side in heaven?" Jesus replied, "the best one here is the one who serves the best."

3. You're faithful. Anyone can start well. How you continue is what makes you worthwhile as a Christian.

4. You obey. Don't give in to the peer pressure of being thought of as a goody-two-shoes-teacher's-pet-know-it-all. If you're simply obeying the Lord, keep it up.

5. You're attentive. Attentive people get a lot more. You're not funny if you're always falling asleep, always messing around, or always making jokes.

6. You learn. Attentive people learn a lot more. Learners win at everything. They figure out what it takes to win, and they can't soak up enough of what will help them.

7. You grow. Attentive learners can't help but grow. They're constantly figuring out what they need to fix in their lives, constantly working on fixing them, and they consequently grow. These points apply to more than just

your spiritual life.

8. You love God. Loving God deeper than anything else changes everything. It changes your Facebook, your speech at school, your shyness about Christ, your church attendance... Do you ever stop and think about Christ and His sacrifice? Love God.

9. You love others. You're NOT the best when you put them down, talk badly about them or talk ugly to them. You're best when you stand up for others, reach out to others, and generally try to help others.

10. You do right. If you love God and you're actively trying to love others, it changes the things you do. If you are just trying to do what's right, don't worry about what others think. Just do right. Do what God would want you to do.

7 Filters To Find God's Will

When your life is not clearly laid out in Scripture, then what? Go through this list of ways to know God's will...

• **God's Word.** First, know it's from God. You're in God's will when you obey God's Word. If it's against the Bible, it's against God.

• **Delighting in God.** Don't make a decision at a time in your life when you're not delighting in God. Psalm 37:4 Let God be the one who puts His desires on your heart.

• **Seeking godly counsel.** Proverbs 1:1-9 are some of my favorite verses. They say, "Son. You don't know anything. Listen to me as I teach you this book of Proverbs." It's very presumptuous to make decisions that go against your godly authorities like church and family (pastor and parents).

• **Praying.** Constantly be praying about your decision. Pray for wisdom and enlightenment. Pray for wisdom for your counselors. Pray humbly, like Daniel. Pray that

God softens your heart for an answer you might not want to hear.

- **Holy Spirit.** The Holy Spirit won't lead every literal step you take, but he is with you at all times and wants you to hear from God. Never ignore His promptings, and learn to hear His voice.

- **Circumstances/fingerprints.** Sometimes God leads through circumstances, but don't take every little opportunity and think, "This is what God wants me to do." Satan can open doors for you, too, and he might be giving you something good when God wants you to have the best. Learn to know when God is opening and closing doors.

- **God's Word.** Always go back to the BEST counsel: God's Word. James 4 makes it clear. Don't be presumptuous and think you have your life figured out. You might have plans, but always be open to Him changing them. Follow God. Do HIS will and you'll be happier than anything else you'd want to do.

Recommended Reading - A List of 16 Books For Every Level Of Reader

Reading has been on my mind lately. Are you a reader? You should be. It's much better for your brains than video games. When I was in high school, I read a bunch of fiction. In college, I moved to non-fiction. Now, most of my reading is non-fiction, and my shelves are full of helpful books. If you ever want to borrow any, please let me know. I'm serious. I hope you become readers. I brought a few samples tonight. Many of my books are written by people who do not believe exactly like us, but they have good points that we can learn from...

- *Biblical Preaching* by Haddon Robinson. It's good if you're into preaching and Bible Study. It shaped my thinking on preaching God's Word, and is a required read at Heartland for the men.

- *Living By the Book* by Howard Hendricks. It's a book on Bible study written for everyone, not just pastors. It is easy to understand and breaks down Bible study very simply.

- *My Journey to Biblical Preaching* is the story of Bro. Sam Davison's change from being a hard-nosed preacher to a Bible preacher. He tells the story of learning how to preach God's Word and how he desires to teach the young men of Heartland to preach.

- *America in Crimson Red* by James Beller. It's a book on Baptist History in America and details the sacrifices of Baptists to shape what America is today.

- *The Calvary Road* by Roy Hession is a short book that dives deep into spiritual self-examination.

- *Spiritual Leadership* by J. Oswald Sanders has been a "textbook" for leaders for a long time. It is deep and will make you think introspectively. You'll read it and feel very... small. ☺ That's good.

- *Spiritual Leadership...* The Interactive Study by Henry and Richard Blackaby is a question/answer type format book on leadership. It examines a lot of Bible and asks compelling questions for the reader to answer.

- *The 7 Habits of Highly Effective People* by Stephen Covey is the book that everybody who's anybody reads. It's a classic. There's a teen version that is really good, but this version just takes you a little deeper.

- *How To Read Better and Faster* by Norman Lewis is a book on speed-reading. It has charts that help you not only read faster but also comprehend what you're reading so you actually get it! It helped me improve my read times by about 30 wpm within a few days of doing the drills.

- *Just Friends* by Cary Schmidt and Mike Ray is a detailed

book on relationships. It is an expanded version of my *A Case For Dating God's Way* booklet, and it will give you lots of Bible principles on dating.

- *Seven Royal Laws of Courtship* by Pastor Jerry Ross is a booklet that gives several Bible principles on dating.

- *Stay in the Castle* by Pastor Jerry Ross is a story for teen ladies who are waiting for God's timing in marriage. Mrs. Jamie read this in one of the split classes.

- *The Teenage Years of Jesus Christ* by Pastor Jerry Ross is a Bible study and series of principles from Jesus' time on earth as a teenager.

- *The Far Side* by Gary Larson. You can borrow my comic books if you're into them. ☺

- *Drawing Cartoons*. If you're into doodling.

- *Sherlock Jones and the Missing Diamond* by Ed Dunlop is a fiction mystery book written for older kids/younger teens. Even though they were written younger, I read all my Ed Dunlop books a couple times each all through high school. They're entertaining.

Readers are leaders. Leaders are readers. Cool people are readers. Bro. Garrett can't read. Bro. Garrett's not cool. (Poor guy. He's not even here to defend himself!)

Try Giving Half

Make the next year a growing year for you. If some of you dedicated HALF the time you spend on video games to reading or listening to audiobooks, you'd be a changed person.

- If you listen to preaching HALF the time you listen to music, you'd be a changed person in 2014.

- If you prayed HALF the time you watch TV, you'd be a new Christian.

- If you read your Bible HALF the time you read fiction or

other reading material, you'd be far more enriched.

- If you spent HALF the time serving at church that you do sitting at home bored, you'd be more fit physically and more fulfilled spiritually.

- If you gave to missions HALF the money you spend buying yourself food, drinks, or other stuff, you'd dramatically notice the difference in your giving spirit.

- If you surrendered HALF of ALL your thoughts to God, you would notice an astounding transformation in your spiritual-mindedness.

- If you gave HALF the attention to preaching that you do to the girl or boy you'd like, God would radically change your life.

If you're honest, you'll notice that HALF of a lot of things in your physical life is still more than ALL of some things in your spiritual life. Some things you can't help... like sleep. You're going to sleep 8 hours per day or so. You're probably not going to read your Bible or serve at church 8 hours per day, but what CAN you do for HALF the time (4 hours)? Think about it. Then purpose to do it.

Do right.

Tips and Tools of Financial Basics

All month leading up to our stewardship Sunday we have heard God's perspective on money: how to get it, how not to get it, how to give it, how to save it, and how to spend it. We have learned that the topic of money is important to God, so it should be stewarded well.

When we think of our lives as though we are not the owner, it changes everything. It's a criminal offense for, say, a mutual fund manager to use the money he's managing to buy himself a nice house! Likewise, to use *our* money (and our lives!) as though WE are the owners is, to God, robbery, according to Malachi.

So when we use God's money, we should be especially careful about *how* we use it. The men in the previous weeks have done a great job showing us God's thoughts from His Word.

Today, we wrap up the 4-week series with fewer Bible verses (although these are biblical principles) but a few tips and tools of financial basics. The most basic categories of all are INCOMING and OUTGOING:

INCOMING

There are a few ways to get money coming in: taxes, stealing (is that the same?), welfare, and work. Do the last one.

A few months ago, I gave these tips to the Teens of Faith. Maybe boosting your income involves the following ideas:

- Work extra jobs
- Get more education: Online college, read books, listen to courses or podcasts, research new ideas online

JOB IDEAS:

- Window cleaning – door to door or businesses. $30 startup costs.
- Baby sitting – Dave Ramsey's daughter – resume, case studies, full report on why she would be the most dependable
- Curb painting
- Lawn mowing
  - Advertise. Make signs and handouts. Pass them around your neighborhood – ask the old ladies in your street if you can do any weeding for them.
  - And then give them tracts
- Sell stuff on Ebay – junk around the house, garage sales, etc.
- Teach yourself graphic or web design – stick a sign in

your yard.

- Pet cleanup services – making rounds every other day for $5/week (or $3/week for one day). Stack up clients and carry a bucket and shovel around. Offer discounts for multiple animals. Include cat litter changing, too. Search online for other services similar.

- Hang flyers on doors

- Washing cobwebs off houses

- Menu planning service

- Grocery delivery – if you live within walking distance of a store

- Dog-walking

- Garage sale/cleaning help – advertise yourself

- Crochet animals and sell them on etsy or ebay

OUTGOING

To accomplish this section, you have to know what is happening with your money. A budget isn't a bad thing—it's a way to know what's happening. It can be low tech (all cash), mid, or high tech (all online).

Give. The tithe (10%) comes first, then you budget the rest. In the Scripture, the word *giving* is always *in addition to* the tithe (i.e. Stewardship commitment, missions, Easter offering, etc. For example, I know a pastor who tithes 10% and gives an additional 20% to missions.)

Save. Know SHORT term and LONG term needs. Don't let summer camp or Christmas surprise you (short term); and plan for new roofs, new AC units, new cars and retirement (long term).

Spend. My favorite section! USE the money God has given you! You're allowed to use it on yourself and your family. My family uses both online spending (for bills) and the cash system for everything else: grocery, fast food, restaurants, gifts, amusement, Ryan (my favorite), and Jamie. When the cash runs out, we wait until next month!

TOOLS

Budget: Mint.com, EveryDollar app, Cash system – lazy man's way! [?]

Books: *Smart Money, Smart Kids*; *My Total Money Makeover*; *The Millionaire Next Door*

TIPS

- **Work** to make good money. America is still the land of opportunity. There's *plenty* of money to be made.

- **Give** off the top. Then do your budget.

- **Start** an emergency fund. Start with $1000 to bail you out of little things, then get out of debt.

- **Eliminate** debt. All of it as fast as you can. Don't spend what you don't have.

- **Know** what you're spending. Call it budgeting, tracking, or whatever-ing. Know that a weekly $7 Starbucks run costs $28/mo. or $350/year!

- **Save** a *bigger* emergency fund (after debt is eliminated). If you lost your job and had $0 income, save enough money to live on for at least 3 months.

- **Save** for big purchases. Cars, house upgrades, kids college, retirement.

- **Plan** for the future. Think about your goals and plan now how to get there: invest in mutual funds or pay off your house, for example.

- **Give** generously from God's blessings (2 Cor. 8-9).

Church

Christian teens will not grow without being in church. Church is God's supernaturally designed place to assemble with fellow believers and worship the Father and learn more of Him. When a teen starts to slip away from church, everything else fails, too.

We work hard at helping teens understand the reasons why we have church, what we are to be and do as church members, and what type of church we should be involved in. These notes address these topics in various forms.

Practical Principles from Hebrews 10 on Attending Church

I'm willing to admit that my views on attending church are based on my upbringing, but I still think they're solidly based on Scripture, according to what I studied preparing for last Sunday's sermon. Growing up, nothing got in the way of church. I mean... nothing! It's weird, I know. But that's how it was for me.

I had soccer practice on Wednesdays. The peer pressure was there—I was concerned about getting made fun of from my friends on the team, but my mom always picked me up early and we went to church. Sunday tournaments were just, "Too bad; we've got something more important that day—church." On vacation, we attended church for every service. And I learned to like it!

Hebrews is the answer to all the pictures of Leviticus. Jesus is our High Priest. When we're taking advantage of the access we have to God's throne, the author commands the reader of Heb. 10: 19-25 to 1) Have full assurance of FAITH, 2) Live in light of our HOPE, and 3) LOVE one another enough to provoke love and good works from each other.

Alone, this is impossible, so in God's infinite genius, he encourages (commands, actually), the regular assembly of like-minded believers to help each other out. This is referring to nothing but church, and the GOAL of this text is to HELP you! Not beat you over the head with more "stuff" to do. Like it's a drudgery. Or a pain.

Church is meant to be a place to encourage your spiritual growth, and for you to help each other, too. So, when we miss out on church, it's only hurtful to us.

24 *And let us consider one another to provoke unto love and to good works:*

25 *Not forsaking the assembling of ourselves together, as the manner of some is; but exhorting one another: and so much the more, as ye see the day approaching.*

Here are a few practical ways to view your church attendance:

1. **See forsaking the assembly like God sees it**: as an abandonment of him. If we saw it like that, we'd be less flippant with services, I think. Research the word *forsake* on your own, and see how seriously God views this: Deut. 28:20; 31:16; 32:15, 18; Judg. 2:12, 13, 20; 10:10, 13; 1 Sam. 8:8; 12:10, etc. See 2 Tim. 4:10, 16.

2. **Admit that the warning is at least valid:** that forsaking the encouragement of the Word at LEAST opens you to the possibility of apostasy. The text following Heb. 10:25 is about those who slip away from truth into false doctrine. You may not fall into apostasy, but you have to admit that the probability is higher when you forsake the regular assembly of the encouragement of the Word (Heb. 13:22).

3. **Instill the habit even when you don't see immediate fruit.** Maybe it's holding TOO strongly to a principle, but I think sometimes we need to be extra-

aggressive with our PRINCIPLES even when they're not Gospel. If anything just to make sure they stay strong, we will do things that may not make immediate sense. That's why we're hanging onto our service structure, why we're having church on Christmas, why we're adamant about not canceling services for every little thing (like Super bowl!), and why Pastor always makes a point to mention what church he attended on vacation. Someone might say, "Well, it was a lame church, and I didn't get anything out of it." There are some things in life that aren't for the MOMENT, but for the LIFETIME.

4. **See church as a COMMITMENT, and not a RIGHT.** Don't treat church as if YOU get to decide which services are going to be beneficial, and which are not. You don't know. You aren't omniscient (all-knowing). Someone might say, "Well it's my RIGHT to go to church." Actually, it's kind of like a place that has its expectations. In the series "I Am a Church Member?" we distinguished between a COUNTRY CLUB and a CHURCH. One (country club) – pay your dues, GET what you can. Other (church) – you give of yourself for the benefit of others.

5. **Expect God to CHANGE YOU in EVERY service**. Come to church expecting to hear from God. He'll speak to you. If anything, the Word of God is preached – that IS God speaking. Even if you like nothing else (and hopefully that's not the case), come to hear the Word!

6. **Keep the kingdom first.** Remember the Sermon On the Mount: "Take no thought..." (Mat. 6:25, 31, 34) Instead, *"seek ye first the kingdom of God, and his righteousness; and all these things shall be added unto you." (v. 33)*

7. **Sincerely analyze your heart motives for missing.** If you say, "It's no big deal," why? Are you tired? Do you have homework? Is it your job? Do you need sleep? Is your schedule too busy? *(See #6 for some*

good thoughts on that.)

8. **Separate excuses from reasons.** If you honestly analyze your reasons in light of God's Word, perhaps your reasons may look more like excuses. There is almost always someone who is older, or works later, or wakes up earlier, or is sicker or has more work than you; yet *they* can make it to church. Are you giving Bible reasons or excuses for missing church?

A "Hellfire and Brimstone" Church In SoCal

This note followed a few weeks of preaching on God's authority in church...

According to what we believe the Bible is teaching us, we can boldly (but not arrogantly) say that since 1987, our church has been serving the Temecula Valley in God's perfect will. Thank God for allowing us to be a part of SUCH a great work! Not only are we a part of a great institution (the church), but we're a part of Calvary Baptist Church—an exciting and unique church in this area!

In some places of America, every corner has an old-fashioned church that with good Bible preaching. That's not true around here! We have people visit us all the time that basically say, "Wow... hymns and 'hellfire and brimstone' preaching... I like it! It's a place that still feels like church!"

I like that. I think God likes that. If He didn't, he wouldn't have put that stuff in His Word.

Do right.

(Yep, Still Missing You) Having a Biblical Mindset About Committed Church

Attendance (Like the Military)

I was vacationing in Central California and wrote this...

Every time we go on vacation we always make it a point to never miss church. This time, when we were planning, we almost couldn't find a church, and finally spotted one about an hour away! It certainly won't be like home with our "family" though.

Do you think that's too far to drive to church? A couple thoughts on that...

1. Maybe someone from the Teens of Faith should go start a church in Central California some day.

2. Maybe a lot of people would say, "Nah. Let's just skip church tonight. It's too far!"

I hope you don't take such a low view of church as if it can be skipped any time you feel like it. Make church a priority in your life. NEVER miss it, unless you're deathly ill.

You want my opinion? No, Bro. Ryan. You're not even here... you shouldn't be allowed to share your opinion. Well you don't have to read on if you don't want... ☺

My opinion is that too many people come up with too many LAME excuses for missing church! Sick? Come on! Tired? Please! Didn't feel like it? Now you're being wicked! ☺

If you ever study the military or watch shows on what some of those guys go through the get into their special forces, it sure is amazing what a proper mindset about what they're doing will push them to do. Those guys absolutely kill themselves for the things they believe in. Would you do that?

"I'm sick. I'm tired." What you're saying is, "God doesn't matter to me near as much as some patch on the sleeve of the Rangers, SEALS, or Air Rescue Team matters to them."

I LOVE that our military men are proud of what they do. Are you that committed?

Choose to be.

Man! Now I want to come home and preach that! ☺ We love and miss you. Do right until we return. (Oh yeah, and after that, too!)

When the Youth Group Looks Different From the Church

This note was just before our TIMELESS Preaching Rally, a 3-session youth rally on one topic...

The Preaching Rally this year has the potential to impact whole churches. We are encouraging the teens to not push the line when it comes to choosing between timeless or trendy.

When I go on another church's website, usually the first place I'll look is at their staff pictures. Next, I'll go to their youth pages and look for pictures. It's always interesting to me to find out what other youth groups do and what kind of activities and programs they have.

Sometimes I'll see a youth group that looks like a totally different church! There are crazy banners on the wall, guitars in the corner, a drum set, punk-looking kids portrayed as the godly examples and other crazy pictures. The rest of the church looks like a fired-up, independent, soul-winning, King James Bible, preaching-loving Baptist church. Probably in 20 years (or sooner!) these solid churches with entertainment-focused youth groups will turn into entertainment-focused churches.

So often, it starts with the youth. If YOU can learn to be passionate about being timeless rather than trendy, it's a whole different ballgame. What if YOU were the ones who were always trying to raise the bar, have higher standards, and glorify God more than self! What if it wasn't coming from your youth director but from YOU? How amazing would it be to see the youth group being the ones who are passionate about soul-winning, about the King James Bible, and about passionately singing doctrine-rich hymns!

Anchor yourself to God's Word and you will be timeless. It's that simple. Timeless, or trendy? It's your choice. Choose timeless... it's just better that way. You'll see why next Saturday.

This article is in reference to the 2013 Preaching Rally theme "TIMELESS."

Why Come To Church?

Why come to church?

- Because your parents make you?
- Because it's fun?
- To hang out?
- For friends?
- Because you always have?

What's the reason? Is it to learn and apply truth? Is it because you love preaching? Is it because you love God's people and you're encouraged by godly friends? Is it because you are enriched by godly music and love to fellowship with other believers? Is it because you love to reach out and help others?

If you were reading through this list and thinking about how someone else might be answering these questions, what are you doing to help them? Are you being that friend? Are you the one encouraging? Are you the reason some people come to church?

That's good! But always remember to point yourself and others to the real reason we come to church.

Still Convinced

I am still convinced that church attendance is a large part of your Christian growth. It is not just about receiving, though. It is also about giving.

I am still convinced that when you serve, you grow. It is amazing to me that when you give of yourself, God renews your energy. Church is a wonderful place to give to others through serving in the music ministry, the food ministries and any other ministry you can involve yourself in.

I am still convinced that the Bible is all you need to live a fulfilled, healthy, refreshed Christian life. I am still convinced that when you ignore the Bible, it shows on your face. I am still convinced that when you ignore the Bible, it shows in your sad spirit.

I am still convinced that giving of your money is more about your heart than it is about the money. God wants you to be obedient to Him, not because of any value you can bring to Him (Luke 17:10), but because of the value He will bring to you.

I am still convinced that most people are unhappy in life because they are disobedient to Christ. I am still convinced that the happiest, most fulfilled people are the ones who are striving to please God in their lives. People who are serving God still have problems in their lives, but they don't have to handle them alone.

The most stressed out, sad people I see are not the ones who have a genuine relationship with God. Think about people like Bro. Beckum and Bro. Bagley... sad and depressed? Angry? Upset? Nope. Not even close.

Joyful. Happy. Excited. Encouraging. Helpful to others. I'm still convinced it takes a real relationship with God to be a real blessing to others. Without God, there's no fruit of the Spirit (love, joy, peace, longsuffering, gentleness, goodness, faith, meekness, temperance).

Do You Want Extra Help In Your Spiritual Life? Try Midweek Church

I'm a big fan of church. It's a helpful place.

It's like GOD designed it or something. Oh wait! He did! THAT'S Why it's so good!

Our church has services on Wednesdays. Some churches do, some churches don't. There is no commandment that says we HAVE to have church on Wednesdays. There is not a verse in the New Testament that talks about how many church services to have.

Scriptures leave those decisions up to the church. What does the leadership think is a wise decision? Would a midweek service HELP people?

Our Pastor thinks it will. Our midweek service is designed to help you grow closer to God. It is meant to be a blessing to you. It is a teaching time that will challenge you to be and do more for God. Is that ever a bad thing?

In life, we should be constantly striving to be better—better students, husbands, wives, children, siblings, friends, etc. We should always strive to get better in every realm—physical, mental, emotional and spiritual.

What is the most important of those? Your body? Your mind? Your emotions? Or your spirit?

Hopefully the answer is obvious. Your spirit.

Do you want help in your spiritual life? One way you can be helped is to come to church on Wednesdays. Guess what we are studying? We are studying how to read and understand your Bible. Well, what does that do? It helps you even more! It helps you nourish yourself spiritually instead of always relying on others to feed you.

Feeling like a weak Christian? Is the world beating you up throughout the week? Coming to church on Wednesdays isn't THE answer, but it sure is a nice tool to help you! Love God. Love others. Do right.

Let's Talk About Church

The preacher summed it up pretty well a couple weeks ago when he said that the church's mission is simple: see people saved, baptized and discipled, and then go start more churches like ours.

That's it.

Honestly. That's all!

And that responsibility does fall on the church, not on any other organization.

The Great Commission focuses on the word *power*. "All **power** is given unto me..." This **power** is not strength, or energy (i.e. "I had enough energy to go door-knocking today!") This **power** is actually **authority.**

Matthew wrote about Christ's authority to conduct ministry, because, to his Jewish audience, authority was a big deal. The Jews were astonished at his doctrine, because He spoke as one having **authority** (7:29). Matthew showed Christ's **authority** to preach (4:17), over nature (8:23-27), over interpreting the Law (ch. 5-7), over sickness and sin (ch. 8-9, stories of healing and forgiveness), over traditions (ch. 9), over the Sabbath (ch. 12), and on and on.

When confronting Jesus, the Jewish leaders never denied Jesus' **effectiveness**. They DID, however, question his **authority**. To them, proper **authority** was needed in order to conduct legitimate ministry. Mat. 21:23, *"And when he was come into the temple, the chief priests and the elders of the people came unto him as he was teaching, and said, By what **authority** doest thou these things? and who gave thee this **authority**?"*

When Jesus cast the demons out of the man in Mat. 12:22, the crowd was shocked. The religious leaders had no explanation. Knowing that Jesus was **effective**, they tried to discredit Him by questioning his **authority**, *"This fellow doth not cast out devils, **but by Beelzebub** the prince of the devils. [emphasis added to show that they accused Jesus of getting his **power*** *for miracles from the devil]"*

They claimed that without proper **authority** (i.e. if Jesus' power DID come from the devil), the miracles would be worthless.

Jesus agreed. (ha!)

Jesus then showed them that devils don't cast out devils, so He must have some higher power (or authority) to conduct His ministry. The point is, Jesus accepted their premise (that authority is needed to minister), and showed that HE had the authority.

Interesting, huh?

Jesus was MORE interested in **authority** than **effectiveness.**

Knowing this doctrine should affect how we live—more devoted to His church.

Every Church Service Is Needed

I don't know if I'd say that every church service is *crucial* to your spiritual walk, but I would say that they are all needed.

Every Sunday school, Sunday morning, Sunday night and Wednesday night service of our church is unique and gives you *something* good. I mean... something! At least *something* spiritually helpful is said or done *every* time we meet together.

On Sundays, the Word of God is preached.

Multiple times.

Have you ever thought of this... you'll *never* know what God *would have* done in your life if you had been in a service you missed. Home playing video games? At the mall? Out with friends? You'll never know if God wanted to do something amazing in your life.

I've told you before that I approach every Sunday school as if the sermon *that day* will be life-changing.

Seriously!

I really think every Sunday: "If they'll get *this* today, then their lives will be changed." So I study and prepare to preach with that goal in mind: life change.

Does it always happen? Nope. Guess when it will NEVER happen...

It will NEVER happen to the person that's not there to hear it.

Every church service is important. Every time God's Word is opened, it can help you.

I talked last Sunday about not coming to church all-Mr.-Grouchy-Pants. I mentioned that we should come expecting to worship our Saviour. You know, the One who died to save us from our sins.

When you come to church, expect to hear from God. Expect to be changed. It starts with something easy... come! I hope tonight is a help to you once again.

Church Won't Cure Face Warts, But...

You'd be awesome if you came to class on Wednesday nights. Yup. Awesome.

Those who came last week are awesome. The guys especially.

We played a version of tic tac toe and the guys won. Oh yeah. Sorry ladies.

So anyways... come this Wednesday night. I hope you make God a priority in your life (like the very first commandment tells us!). God should come first in every area of your life, but He usually gets pushed around by the schedule. I love those of you who would NEVER miss church for anything.

That says a lot about you. It means your priorities are straight. It means you have a lot of other things right in life.

I'm not saying there's something wrong with you—like you'll grow warts all over your face or something—if you miss church.

I'm just saying that it's right to keep God first, and He desires you to be in church. That's all I'm saying.

So what about coming this Wednesday? Ask your parents. Tell them God told you to come. See what they say. ☺ I love you teens. Do right.

Staying With True Doctrines

I went to West Coast's graduation today, and Pastor Chappell preached a powerful message to the students about sticking to the same doctrines that they've learned all through college.

Now that I'm away from college, I see the allure of the world. I see the pressures of other ministries. I see the stress of standing for pure doctrine. I see the firm stand that is very unpopular in this world.

NOW I see why preachers preached like that when I was in college. Because they've been down the road and can see further than I can. NOW I get it.

I'd be wise to get it. That's why I'm careful about my music, movies, Bible, and philosophy of ministry. I don't have all the answers, but I'm trying to follow people that have struggled through the same questions I have. I want to learn from their wisdom.

It's easy to think I know better than the "old timers." But I'm a fool if I neglect their wisdom. I need them. I need to always be reminded to focus on pure doctrine.

How about you?

Discipline

The Christian life is a life of discipline. Every Christian principle works... if you do it. Doing it takes effort. Usually daily effort. That's hard! It takes discipline.

Perhaps one of the biggest problems I see in teens today is a lack of discipline. Teens tell me that they love God, but few of them show it in how they live.

These articles encourage teens to be more disciplined by showing examples, giving practical tips, or generally calling them to more discipline.

God Can Use Teens To Bring Revival... If They're Disciplined

I really believe God can use our youth group to bring revival. If you carry on what God did in your heart at camp, you can't help but spread that fire.

Jehu started great, but he

1. Didn't give up sin, and
2. Disregarded God's law.

Don't let that be you. Stay close to God. Have a passionate hunger to learn from God's Word.

When I was a freshman or sophomore and really started "getting it" spiritually, I bought books, I read devotionals on my own, I asked questions... basically, I'm saying this: Don't be the type of person that always NEEDS encouragement. Drive yourself. Let God be so real to you that you can't get enough. And do that on your own.

Grow yourself to the point of encouraging others rather than always needing encouragement. God wants to do something with you, and he will if you let Him.

With school starting this week, let God shine through your life, so that you can be salt and light. Pray for us... we're praying for you!

Here Lies a Deceased iPod's Ashes

At a youth bonfire at the beach after camp, we cremated a teen's iPod. This was the followup note the next day...

Once full of garbage music.

Now mortified.

Would you be that intense about YOUR sin? When Dylan gave his testimony a couple months ago, he mentioned the music he listened to when he was younger, and last Sunday we had a funeral service for his old iPod. Christian teen, WHATEVER it is in your life that's holding you back, get it out. Mortify it. For good.

Mortification is about RADICAL change that shows. Some of you that SAID you changed your heart still need to "manifest" some change like that on the outside. Help each other out!

- Wake each other up when your buddy's nodding off

- Amen the preaching and your buddy will too

- Help keep your guy/girl friend's mind on the preaching by not getting too close to him/her... add your Bible as a "spacer" to ensure you don't touch. Or... do that for your friends.

- Sit up front

- Give a testimony when asked what God's doing in your life ("let the redeemed of the Lord say so," otherwise it seems like God's NOT working on you!)

- Take some tracts home tonight and plan how you'll pass

them out tomorrow

You're as close to God as you want to be right now, and the fulfilling, beautiful, matchless, joyful Christian life is found in DISCIPLINED OBEDIENCE to God. Love God, yes; but don't let it stop there. Let that love GROW you in Him.

We're sure blessed to be with you, and we pray so often that you'll be good testimonies at your schools and in your neighborhoods. Just this week again it was SO encouraging to see some of you get some GOOD music, and others of you even going so far as dropping a class that might hinder your spiritual life!... Wow! God is good!

Is He good enough to you to make some "radical" changes? Well, of course HE is good enough. Do YOU see Him that way? I hope so. He's only saved you from... sin... hell... condemnation. No big deal?

Love God. Love others. Do right.

What's Your Plan So Far? Your "Decision" Is a Lie Until This Happens

What did you do last Sunday that was different from the Sunday before? You need to think about what ZEAL might look like!

During the:

- Preaching – maintain eye contact. Look excited. Look up! Listen. Say "Amen!" Get right up close to the preaching. Read the text ahead of time. DON'T TALK with your friends. Don't distract guy/girl friends by sitting too close or "accidentally" touching. Keep a pure and concentrated mind

- Singing – sing! Concentrate on the words. Let the words mean something to you; don't just sing them. Open your mouths! Don't "drift off" and look at the light bulbs again... they're not THAT interesting! Oh yeah and...

SING

- Fellowship time – greet people. Shake everyone's hand. Search for guests in the main service (there are always new teens in the back.) Talk to people. Encourage people. Invite them to activities. Discourage bad speech or bad attitudes. Talk to people that you don't know.

You can say all you want that you're "on fire" and things are different, but it's all a lie until it's seen. All we have to go on is what you do, not what you say.

I'm not saying at ALL that you are all liars! I'm just going to always be the voice that pushes you to always "step it up."

You'll never "arrive," but it's more about the journey than the destination, anyway! Do right. Love God. Love others.

Purpose To Improve By 10% In Key Areas

This note was from the first day of the new year...

Happy New Year!

I hope you work VERY hard today to stay engaged... especially if you were up last night shooting illegal fireworks off at midnight.

Last year at this time, Pastor preached a sermon called, "Purposes. Not Resolutions." New Year's Resolutions are great, but purposes are more enduring.

This time of year is a time to think BACK on the past year and FORWARD on the coming year. As we think on the Teens of Faith, consider how well you've done in the past, and maybe make some improvements for the future:

- Be Our Guest involvement
- Saturation Saturday attendance
- Heart for service
- Spirit to give

If you could improve yourself by 10% in each of these areas, what would you change? Would a 10% improvement mean that you greet every guest? Or start coming to Saturation Saturday? Or be the first to volunteer to set up chairs? Or talk to your parents about helping you make sure you have $1/week?

These are just a few areas. Ask yourself how to improve, and ask God's help.

We sure love you! God's way is ALWAYS best. Do right.

Is It Persistence or Faithfulness?

It seems like everyone out there puts a big emphasis on persistence, right?

"Don't ever give up."

That's the mindset. "You can do anything you set your mind to." Never hold back; give everything your all.

People are so passionate about persistence and dedication, and they're devoted to so many different things. Some people are so passionate about sports, about dance, about grades, about their college choice... about everything!

The Bible has preached that same message forever, only the Bible term is faithfulness. I find it strange when someone thinks that he or she is a persistent person that "never gives up" and "always pushes hard at everything" but never takes that same passion to the things of God.

You should be more impressed with someone who is faithful to God for a lifetime than you are with some star athlete's workout routine. People's persistence is only as deep as their faithfulness. If you've ever made a promise or a commitment to God, stick to that before wandering off on any other tangent. Be sure to be more persistent in godly things than you are in anything else in life.

Be faithful to church! It matters far more than anything else in life. Come tonight. Come on Wednesday. Be faithful to your commitment to be in play practice (we had a LOT gone last week!) Just be faithful. God will bless that above all else!

How Bored Do You Get?

We host a one-day 3-session youth rally each year. This note explained one of our themes...

The Preaching Rally theme this year is Timeless.

The concept behind Timeless is that every Christian will benefit when he learns that there is much more meaning to the time-tested and proven things in life than there is in the trendy, new and flashy things.

Timeless or trendy? Which do you prefer?

Most teens prefer trendy, or new things. One sure way to test your appetite for trendy is to ask yourself, "How bored do I get?"

You load a new app, use it a while, then it's old. You search for a new one and maybe even buy it, but the thrill doesn't last. You're bored.

You get new clothes, wear them once, get complimented, wear them again, maybe get a couple more compliments, wear them again and they're old. Then you're bored with it. They're not fresh any more. You need new.

How bored do you get?

You come to church and it's the same thing as always. You sit through the same preacher and play the same games and go on the same activities. Remember when things were exciting to you? Are you bored now?

Devotions can get old, too. You wake up and feel as badly as you did yesterday—your eyes won't stay open and you just want to go back to sleep. You can't concentrate anyway... why read my Bible? BIBS was new and exciting at first... but you've done it a while and now it's not new any more. What will it take for this to be exciting again? I need something fresh. I need something new. Have you ever thought that?

Timeless is all about fighting off that mentality. Being timeless means that you realize some things in life might seem boring, but if you're really thinking about them right, they are the best things in life. Being timeless means that you don't always have to have new things in order to be interested. Church doesn't always have to be a new sermon series or a novel concept. Devotions don't always have to be in a new format. Being timeless simply means that you are not giving in to the constant and never-ending craving for new. After all, you'll never get enough, so why not just do what you know you should do and anchor yourself to God's timelessness. It will last. I promise.

Spiritual Decisions + Spiritual Discipline = Spiritual Growth

This note came after a great day of outreach with our church...

If you were one of the 45 or so who made it to Saturation Saturday, thank the Lord for your presence! I know a lot of you would have been if you could have been, but it was awesome to see so many people act on spiritual decisions that were made a long time ago! Remember camp... **Spiritual decisions + Spiritual discipline = Spiritual growth.**

That's your math lesson for the day (sorry to sneak it in during the weekend)! What a blessing that you desired to serve God through inviting others to our church and telling others about what the Lord has done in your life (remember the story about the Maniac of Gadera from Pastor's sermon last week?) Amen! Keep up the good work!

Till next time! We love you and pray for you more than you'll know.

Make Specific Goals To Follow Up Your Decisions

I try to work on my productivity as much as I can. One book that I found particularly helpful is called Getting Things Done, and a MAJOR step in his process is writing things down.

So I try to write everything down. Phone calls come in, I grab a pen and write down the salesman's name and use it. Someone asks me for something... I pull out a pen and paper and write it down so I won't forget. When I get to my office, especially after a Sunday, I go through all my notes and things to do. I hate forgetting things, and I hate letting people down. Writing it helps me.

One reason you all received a notebook was to help you write things down. Taking notes is a valuable skill to learn, because any time you make a commitment to do something ("Sure, I'll bring that to you next week..."), you obligate yourself to either do it or be a liar. "I forgot." Well, you still lied. ☺

I try to write everything I can down, and I use a little checkbox system. Every time you hear something you need to do, write it down and put a little empty box next to it. When you do it, check-off the box. Simple or huge, write every little step and check it off, one by one.

Don't be too general; be specific. Don't write, "Be thankful," write:

- Ask Bro. Ryan or Bro. Ken to point out Mary Wright
- Thank Mary Wright for the notebooks.
- Write mom and dad a thank-you note.

Write step-by-step goals for yourself. Don't write, "clean up Facebook wall," write:

- Unfriend _____
- Post a Bible
- Delete all posts with profanity
- Revisit my profile page and compare each listing to Phi. 4:8-9

Life is made up of specifics. So get specific and be productive.

Take notes! Write it down. It will help you. Enjoy your books!

Make Your Summer Count. Here's How:

Don't waste your summer.

Too many people waste their summer time on video games and sleep. Don't be lazy.

Have I told you lately that I hate video games?

I don't hate video games directly—I'll play some iPhone games here and there—I just hate that they suck the lives out of people. I hate when they're the things you do when you should be interacting with real people. I hate when you're on mobile games when you should be talking with people at church. I hate when you kill time on video games when you could be reading. I hate when you move colored pixels till 2:30 on Saturday night and then you sleep through church.

I just hate when dumb things get in the way of important things. Oh wait... that's kind of like the first commandment. Ok I'm just being sarcastic now, but it's still true. Video games can easily become a god to you. If you're not willing to take a month or two off, ask yourself, "Why not?" Is it SO important to you that you couldn't live without them? If it's a god to you, drop it. If it's a big deal to drop it, it's probably a god to you. If you're trying to rationalize to yourself why you play so many video games, it's probably a god to you. If it's a god to you, drop it... You get the idea.

Use your summer for God.

- Take your free time as an opportunity to pull weeds at church
- Be at door knocking every Saturday
- Go door knocking with the interns on Tuesdays, Wednesdays and Thursdays at 2:30
- Come to youth activities

- Ride your bike
- Build a shed
- Plan a hike
- Write a book

Seriously. Do something productive this summer. Plan it out. Write it down. Commit to it.

Or waste your time and regret your summer. What I do not want is for you to have regrets. I want you to challenge yourself to be more and do more and accomplish more. You'll be happier with yourself if you accomplish something this summer, so get busy and DO something.

Those of you who are self-motivated won't have any trouble filling your time with productive things to do. Those of you who aren't self-motivated, write down 20 things you want to accomplish this summer and get them done

- Write notes
- Read books
- Learn to write code
- Build a computer
- Cut down a tree
- Split firewood
- Cook a full meal
- Write a sermon

Whatever... Think of something on your own.

I guarantee that all of you could be doing WAY more for the Lord than you're doing now. I know that's true about ME! I just need to stop and think about what I want to accomplish this summer and put a plan in place to do it.

Make your summer count.

Most Excuses For Spiritual Problems Relate To Bad Time Management

I've talked to a couple people lately about time management.

When you think of time in relation to our Proverbs series, ask yourself, "What is the wise thing to do *right now* with my time?" Do you ever think about where your time goes?

A couple years ago at the Youth Winter Rendezvous we did an exercise that had you rate how much time you spent on things. If you were to do it now, my guess is that sleep and school are pretty high up there, and church and godly things might be kind of low (in comparison). But wait... doesn't the Bible tell us "seek ye first the kingdom of God?" Yep.

Seeking God first in things (or, staying on the "path" of wisdom) should influence your schedule. You will put important (eternal) things first in your life.

My wife and I were talking the other day, and we sort of concluded that if our kids were ever involved in anything—soccer, school plays, chess club, anything—that caused us to say, "I hope we can make it to church tonight," they just wouldn't go.

Our stance might seem hardcore, but I think church will always be better than soccer practice. I used to leave soccer practice early every Wednesday night to be in church. I'd change in the car on the way to church, and I would benefit because of it. Sunday tournament games were never even a question. There's no chance I'd be going, because I was going to church.

So, time management is about telling your time what you're going to do with it. Homework to do? That's okay. Don't ignore it. Don't just fail all your classes and think you're somehow "righteous" because you went to church instead of studying for your test. No! Just manage your time better. Study in the 4 hours between school and church, and the 2 hours after church before bed. Study in the morning before school. Here's a thought... study a little bit every day so you don't have to cram.

*gasp!

Time management makes room for the most important things in life. What's important to you will get done. I'm just here to say: Make your spiritual life the most important. "Seek ye first the kingdom of God and his righteousness."

Be Intentional About What You Do

Are you deliberate about what you do? Life is to short to just let it slip by. Eternity is too important to waste time on selfish things. Are you intentionally improving yourself spiritually?

I am not perfect—not even close—but I try to work at being intentional. Each note I write, each sermon I preach, each activity we do... almost everything related to the Teens of Faith is intentionally designed to help you in some way. The pictures on the wall have a reason behind them. The fact that we structure our class times this way is intentional. The times we have special trips are reasoned.

My wife and I think about you all the time. We talk about you. We want to help you, so we intentionally do things to help you.

We do that in our marriage, in our family, and in our ministry. I try to do that in my own personal life, too.

Do you?

Don't just float through life. Please make it mean something!

Be wise. Be *scripturally* wise. Make choices each day that intentionally help you to be more wise.

I love you all! The BEST way I can love you is to help you be a wiser person. Now go wise up!

SEALs Make Time

I've been reading a book by a couple Navy SEALS about leadership and business. It applies not only to leaders, but to everyone who wants to get things done.

One of the SEALs said that the *best* SEALs were those who were the most disciplined. He said it was usually the older, more experienced SEALs who got the most accomplished—they had the neatest weapons, the best uniforms and knew their mission the best. In a SEAL schedule, they leave you NO room to do all the extra stuff, so you have to make the time.

The book covered an entire section on discipline. Coming in from a fierce battle, covered in sweat, exhausted from fatigue and no sleep—these guys still had to fill out paperwork. Then, they'd set THREE alarms—one electric, one battery, and one wind-up—so there were NO excuses for sleeping in the next morning. Wow! I like that. He said that a disciplined SEAL gets up on the FIRST alarm.

The human body is capable of a LOT more than we think it is. SEALs show us that almost every day. They push their body and mind to its limit, and then keep on pushing.

Spiritual warfare deserves every bit as much dedication and drive. Did you read your Bible last week? At all?

Your schedule is what you make it. And it's not all about getting less sleep. That might be part of it, but it's not all of it. Your schedule is yours to control. Don't waste God's time that He's given you. Use it for eternity. If SEALs can make time for whatever THEY want to do, WE should be able to make time for God, right?

Love God, love others, and do right.

After a While, Things Start To Slip

This note helped explain some of the reasons behind the rules...

Have you noticed in your life that if you're not super-deliberate and driven about something, it kind of fades?

I used to be *really* into guitar. I used to be, like, good. Not any more! I've let it slip.

I bet Robbie was better at basketball a month ago than he is today. He's let his skills slip. Psh. Come on, Robbie. (Just kidding. For those who don't know... he messed his leg up a few weeks ago.)

I took Algebra, then Geometry, then Algebra 2. Since I'd taken a year off Algebra to do Geometry, when I got to Algebra 2, my skills had slipped! It was horrible! I felt so dumb.

Over time, things start to fade unless you're really passionate about taking care of them. Too much else in life demands our attention, huh?

Well, with the youth ministry, I want to revisit a few things that have slipped, a little. Nothing bad. Just a few reminders:

1. *Please sit with your parents, or in the youth section for services.* We've had a few slip-ups, distractions, and other stuff that makes me remind you of this now. If you could do that, it would help everyone.

2. *In class, please have only the seniors on the back row.* I'll always allow guests back there if they're more comfortable. But if you're not a senior, please don't put it on me to move you. "He'll tell me to move if he wants me off the back row." No. I probably won't. I'm too scared.

3. *That's all. You guys are doing great.* You're serving. You're singing. You're in church. You're doing GREAT in your BIBS. You're registered for camp. You're reading your *3 Sons* book from Bro. Schwanke. You're coming on door-knocking. Everything's going well. Keep it up.

I love you all. Love God. Love others. Do right.

Can You Believe Summer Is Half Over?

This note was a reminder halfway through the summer to stay intentional...

It feels like we just got out of school, yet we're already halfway through the summer break! We bought the interns' plane tickets, we're planning their last youth activity, camp is only a couple weeks away, and time is FLYING away! Before you know it, school will be starting up again and you'll be too busy for this and that. As if summer time is "not" busy.

If we are not careful with our time, it slips away from us. Leading up to the LA Missions Trip, many of you were in your Bible almost daily. When summer hit, did you keep up that habit? Or have you let it drop away?

If we are not careful, time slips away so fast, that a whole SUMMER goes by without ever thinking about reading our Bibles. We'll think, *"Yeah, I've missed a couple days... maybe a week. hmm. How long HAS it been?? Uh oh. Where'd the time go?! It's AUGUST already?!"*

Time never stops marching on. YOU have to be the one that chooses what you do with time.

Are you redeeming it? Are you using it wisely?

I'm not accusing. Just asking. Use your time to build your love for God, your love for others, and your desire to do right.

After Revival Services

This note followed a 4-day revival service with Bro. Sam Davison...

When the revival services are done, what do you do?

Last week, we had services with my favorite preacher of all time, Bro. Sam Davison. You may or may not have appreciated his ministry, but what we got was God's Word, plain and simple.

Remember Sunday school? I loved the quote, "I've never met anyone who has grown in their walk with God by going to church only one service per week." True!

Or Sunday morning? The wayward heart. The stony ground. Those who hear the Word and don't really care. That was for unbelievers AND Christians. Is that YOUR heart?

Or remember Sunday evening? Or Monday? Or Tuesday or Wednesday? We learned from Zephaniah, from the Sermon on the Mount, from Paul in 2 Corinthians and on and on.

What did you change this week?

Anything?

Or... are you "settled on your lees?" If you missed Wednesday, Bro. Davison preached that's it's easy for God's people to forget God's goodness, ignore His warnings and go through the everyday Christian stuff without knowing or caring what they're doing. That's when life starts to stink, and the "lees" needs to be stirred up to keep the juice sweet and useful.

I'm always fearful for my own walk with God to get old and boring. I have to work to keep it fresh.

You do too.

God tried to shake you up. Did you listen? What have you changed? Anything? How did you grow spiritually last week?

Or did you?

I'm not accusing you. I'm just asking. AFTER revival services, what has improved in your spiritual life?

You Should Grow In Spiritual Things Every Day

Every time you come to church, I hope you're reminded about spiritual things... but what about home?

I hope you're not wasting your time this summer. It's a biblical principle to "redeem the time" while you have it, and I pray that you spend your time on more than video games, sleep and fun. Service, growth, learning—those are things that help you in life, while fun only satisfies you a little.

Hey, I'm not hating on fun... I've been in my parents' pool a lot lately, and swimming isn't necessarily spiritually enriching or mentally challenging! But I've also spent a LOT of time thinking about and praying for you, preparing for camp spiritually, and just generally... growing. I want to CONSTANTLY be growing better in everything I do, from my little computer jobs to the big task of keeping my relationship with the Lord sweet.

How do you use your time? Serve. Grow. Love people. I can't wait till next week!

Why Is It So Hard?

Have you ever wondered, "Why is the Christian walk so hard?!"

I have.

I'll admit it. "Why can't it just be... easy to live right, do right, love people, not get mad, discipline myself..."

I hate not being good at stuff. I hate falling behind, so I hate it when I fall behind spiritually. I just want it to come easy for me.

But it doesn't. It takes work. It takes commitment. It takes faithfulness. It takes discipline. It sometimes stinks.

I wake up early every day. I read. I pray. I study my Bible. I try to control my tongue. I try to discipline my mind. I work on my schedule to make time for family, soul-winning, church ministry, church, and everything else I need to do. I work like crazy to be balanced—not overdoing the DO-ing of the Christian walk but also not neglecting the DO-ing either.

Most people want heaven and a guilt-free life. That's about it.

They want heaven when they die, and when they're alive, they don't want the guilt when they're not obedient to God while they're alive. Is that you? I hope not.

Go all in! You have one foot in the boat and one foot on land, and the boat is floating away! Jump in! Stop trying to straddle both.

Once you're all in, it's actually pretty easy. Christianity stops being hard, because it's no longer something you "have" to do.

If you're asking, "Why is it so hard," maybe you should be

asking, "Am I all in?"

If not, make it easy on yourself. Surrender to God.

Spiritual Maturity

No Christian is perfect, but a mature Christian is constantly growing. These notes talk about some of the areas that are marks of a more spiritually mature Christian.

When Others Receive a Compliment, How Do YOU Respond?

This note came after some 7th graders served in a workday...

"The 7th graders were THE MAN!"

Those were Mrs. Jamie's words on Sunday night after the fundraiser. Obviously, everyone else helped too, and we appreciate that, but from what I saw they were seeing the need and taking the lead... after services AND before with the setup too.

For you non-7th graders: train yourself to have a spirit that never gets upset when someone else is complimented and you're not. Learn to rejoice with those people, and praise God that He's working in all kinds of lives.

All you need to worry about is you, and as long as you're being faithful to everything you should be, God sees it and will bless it.

God sees your work. You know, I always see your work too, but I'm not always able to mention it to you...

Don't be upset if you feel you're overlooked. If you did a good job before God, train yourself to be OK with that and rest in the fact that He saw it and you were obedient to Him. You'll go VERY far in life with that mentality. You live in a thankless world that's always looking for compliments but doesn't want to give them out.

Be an encouragement to others, and rest confidently in God for yourself.

Would You Sit In the Back Row?

If you were given the choice, would you sit in the back row?

Why?

Is it... a better view? No. Control over who can see your back? Stop being paranoid. A spiritual thing? Oh come on, Bro. Ryan... give me a break! How could the seat I sit in be a spiritual thing?! You're crazy! Haha! Maybe I am crazy!

All I'm asking is that you check your heart and motives for everything you do... including the seat you choose.

In most settings when Jr. High and High Schoolers are allowed to sit wherever they want, the jerks sit in the back and are jerks to everyone else. (sorry, seniors... you're not jerks!) ☺ What's so good about the back?

We've added another row of chairs and I hope we can fill it every week! But be careful if you find yourself wanting to gravitate away from authority, from preaching, and from being "close." (you know what I mean?)

A huge goal of mine since coming here has been to see a few of you REALLY get excited about the Lord, His Word, preaching, and everything associated with church! I pray for all of you by name often and want God's best for you! I also keep praying for that goal to be accomplished with YOU (not quite there...), but if we start to see some of you gravitating "away," we will have to make a couple small changes... even changes with the seating.

You might think I'm crazy and paranoid for even bringing this up, but I'd say God's opinion about that matters the most. I'll do anything I can to nurture and grow your zeal for God. Are you willing to do your part?

Sit close. Look up during the preaching. Say "Amen!" (men especially!!) Get the tired looks off your faces. Raise your eyebrows and eyelids and smile, even when you're listening! Excitement and your love for God will show on the outside, so show it intentionally. We love you!

I Want You To Have Jobs You Love Some Day

This note came after we were away on vacation...

Whew! You didn't revolt. Thanks for that!

We're very happy to be back from our vacation, and we are thankful to those of you who prayed for us. All went well with the travels and we had a relaxing and restful time with family and friends. We bragged on you everywhere we went!

I hope you all get jobs some day that you love as much as I do! I hope you obey God now and let Him lead you in His will all along. As long as you're obedient to the Bible, you can't miss His plan for your life. (Read that last sentence again... it's a good one.)

Being a youth pastor is not what's great... doing what God has for me is what's great! If you're obedient to God's Word and are in His will, ANY job you work can often be a joy... for me, it's a job I even look forward to getting home from vacation to work! I love that!

Bro. Ken told me that I would have been proud to see you last week with our "Be Our Guest" stuff. I wish I could have seen it, but it sure sounds like you're acting on what you know to do... that's a great step.

Finally, thank you so much for our picture on Wednesday! We

happened to be at a restaurant with 2 other youth pastors and their wives, and we were SO happy to show them all your pretty little faces. We love you, teens.

Let Jesus Be Lord of the Realm

This note came after a youth activity at a church member's house...

How have you "let Jesus be the Lord of your realm" this week?

Have you made any spiritual changes? If you haven't GROWN in Christ this week, does that mean you are backslidden? Did you read your Bible on Monday morning? Or did you lazily drag out of bed at noon, play video games and then jump in the pool? You can say all you want that you love God, but HE won't believe it until He sees it in action. Don't be caught up in what He condemns... rather, let His way become your way. I'm already excited about next Sunday's sermon, and I hope you make it to Sunday school on time!

Everyone should thank Mrs. Wyman again for letting us come to her house. (And we should probably apologize to her neighbors for all the yelling! "I'VE BEEN TO NARNIA!") By the way... who did you invite to come to the last Afterglow? Anyone? Who are you GOING to invite to this Sunday's?

I'm talking about spreading the word in Sunday school, "Hey are you coming tonight? You should..." Let's fill up the bus when we go to the Baker's this coming Sunday!

Do right. Love God. Love others. Love me... wait...

God Is All That Will Matter in 3,582 Years

This note followed a beach activity...

If you missed the Beach Bash last Friday, you missed out on not only a good time, good food, and crazy (rough?) games; but a great time of testimonies from lots of the teens who went. John 15 is one of the most encouraging chapters you could read on how to grow as a Christian and how to WIN in life... how to have TRUE joy: 1) Purge the junk, 2) abide in Christ, 3) obey His Word.

I've tried to say it often: "It's simple, but it's not easy!" I promise you it gets easier and "funner" the more you taste of God's goodness. The first steps you take in your spiritual life can SEEM hard, but that's just the flesh fighting you. MORTIFY IT! Kill the flesh till it's extinct!! Then love God. And obey His Word.

I LOVED hearing the testimonies that I got to hear, and my wife filled me in on all the others Friday night when we got home. What a blessing to hear of good friends; standing out, standing up, standing firm even when "friends" turn their backs on you for it; getting rid of music and TV shows; starting the school year off with good classes; and WAY more (including an iPod cremation and a video of another iPod R.I.P.!) I LOVED it! Do you think God loved it? I'm sure He did.

Go crazy on sin. ALL of it. Give your all to God. He's worth it. He's the only thing that will matter in 3,582 years. Your sin will only be regret, and your righteousness will only be joy. Love God. Love others. Do right. We love you and had a GREAT time with you Friday and Saturday!

Learn To See the Spiritual Aspect of ALL You Do

This note followed our church's Vacation Bible School with Evangelist Ed Dunlop...

Did you enjoy the Family Crusade last week?

More than enjoying it, I hope you see the spiritual value to the week. Halfway through the week I had to check my spirit. People were talking about the souls that were saved, and when I wasn't thinking about it, I was more concerned about the songs, the penny offering, the games, the fun... I was wrong!

Please, at ALL times, see the spiritual aspect of everything that you do.

I've used this phrase before: *Think Spiritually.*

About everything.

School. Family Crusade. Guests in class. Homework. Dinner. Everything! Think spiritually. Learn to see God in every minute of every day. That's how Bro. Beckum described prayer... a relationship with Christ.

Thank you for all your great work last week with the Family Crusade! Praise God for how it turned out! Btw... can someone buy me a new toothbrush? Mine is worn out...

These final sentences refer to the losing team captain (me) having to eat peanut butter off the toes of the winner (my wife).

Memorizing Scripture Will Keep You From Sin

Memorizing Scripture, according to Psalm 119:11, helps to keep you from sin. If you abhor sin, like we talked about on Sunday (Rom. 12), you'll do whatever you can to keep from it. Accountability, memorization, reading your Bibles, etc.

Memorizing Scripture is a skill all of you can learn, and all of us should learn! It just takes discipline and work... kind of like anything else worth while in life.

Have a Healthy Dissatisfaction With Your Spiritual Life

What's that mean?!

It means it's okay to not be okay with some things. You should be dissatisfied with certain aspects of your Christian life. I'm not saying you should be discontent, upset or mad... I'm saying you should be healthily dissatisfied.

Never be okay with your **spiritual walk.** The minute you think you're okay, the devil will blindside you. Further, you'll never "arrive" at the ultimate spiritual place... you should always be growing.

Never be okay with our **class growth.** "We have a good amount of people. We don't need anyone else. It's fine how it is." Banish those thoughts from your mind! We can always use more teens in our class, and it will take work! Remember Be Our Guest? Every teen greets every guest. Bro. Ken and I were watching a couple weeks ago and the ladies did well, but the men fell a little short. Everyone should notice guests and greet everyone in class. Also, keep up on the ones who might only come on Sunday mornings.

- Invite them to Wednesdays

- Sit with them

- Make sure they know about activities

- Friend them on FB

Never be okay with how much you **serve.** No one here serves too much. I've been around a lot of churches and I've seen a lot of different types of people. Some people only come on Sunday mornings and think you're crazy for asking them to serve. Other people... you can't keep them away from church they serve so much! There's a whole spectrum of people out there. Be one of those whose whole lives are centered around church. Serve. Do right.

Love God. Love others. Do right.

This Topic Is Scary, But Needed

Servant leadership; that's what. Pastor is a great servant leader.

He is kind, funny, gentle, caring, meek, not in-your-face, and wise. None of these things, though, make him weak, because he has chosen to use those traits as tools to help others in his leadership.

He has chosen, despite personal inhibitions and excuses, to allow God to use him to lead. He could be fairly shy although you'd never see it. He could be more comfortable with just family around although he constantly has guests up to his house. He could be stuffed up in his office all day but he still does all the common projects around church. He's a servant leader.

Servant leaders lead despite the glory. They don't lead because they get the glory. True servant leaders don't want it, and many great leaders are actually shy and embarrassed by the attention they receive. Read the book Good to Great and you'll see that one huge factor to any institution's success is its leader. Even in business, the servant leader model is the best.

Are you a servant leader? I'm not asking if you're able to lead. Nor am I asking if you're a leader. Remember camp last year... are you a good follower? If you are truly a good follower, you should then be transitioning to a position of servant leadership. When your goal is to help others instead of getting attention, you're on the right path.

Servant leaders serve when no one else will. Any good leader will tell you that basically everything he does is scary. Leading means that you're the one putting yourself out there first. You never know how you will be accepted. A good servant leader, though, cares more about doing what he knows has to be done than he does about his image. "It's scary, but if no one is going to step up, I will."

Servant leaders encourage others. The difference between servants and servant leaders is that pesky second word... leader. Anyone can serve. That's the easy part. Who's going to take initiative? Who's going to step up and be the first one out there? Not so he can be noticed, but so he can encourage others in a servant's spirit.

Servant leaders have the right motive. And everyone can sense it. If he's serving just so he can get some attention, no one takes him seriously. If he's truly motivated to be a servant leader, despite being afraid, others will be encouraged by it. If you're burdened about servant leadership, which aspect are you missing? Do you serve but don't encourage others to do the same? Or, do you try to lead but no one really cares because they know you're not a servant and you're just doing it to be noticed?

Servant leaders encourage others. Be encouraging to others. Sometimes all it takes is your example. Sometimes it takes more. Servant leadership doesn't necessarily have age limits, but everyone in our class, including the current 7th graders, will be older than someone when the new 7th graders promote up. Sure, the new 7th graders can be servant leaders, but we're going to focus more on them just becoming servants first. Their leadership development will come later. For now, what about you?

Do Not Fear God's Will—Anticipate It

I think some people are afraid of God's will—like it's something bad.

That's crazy! As if YOU—simple little knucklehead that you are —could out-plan God?!

He knows the thoughts he thinks toward you, and they're GOOD!

Jer. 29:11 For I know the thoughts that I think toward you, saith the Lord, thoughts of peace, and not of evil, to give you an expected end.

Last week's sermon was about that concept, too. Prov. 19:8 says *"He that getteth wisdom loveth his own soul: he that keepeth understanding shall find good."* Do you love yourself? Do you want to do what's best for you? Do you want the GOOD things to come to you?

God wants your best, too.

The ladies sang that song "Consume Me, Lord" a couple weeks ago. It was awesome. I loved it. As I was listening to the song, one of the lines moved me. It was something like, "If you're struggling with surrender, do not be afraid of his call on your life."

Are you struggling with surrendering? Is Christ at the center of your life? Are you consumed by Him? Are you eager to do His will? Do you anticipate it, or fear it? Are you excited by God's will, or scared of it?

His way is best. I guarantee it. Psh. Who cares about what I say... GOD guarantees it. Take HIS Word for it.

Love Is In the Air

This note came after a wedding of two of our church members...

Aw, how sweet.

The wedding yesterday was a good reminder of the "why" behind the biblical commandments to be pure. Save yourself for marriage. It may be tough, but God's way is always best.

Every time I'm at a wedding, I am reminded of my own. How could I not be, right? Sure, the girls get more thrill out of weddings, but guys can take something away from them, too. Guys can see marriage as the biblical goal of dating. I did. I loved my own wedding (it's about the only wedding I've ever loved.) When dating is done God's way, it is a huge blessing. When marriage is the goal and God is the focus, dating is a time of spiritual growth rather than fleshly lust.

Our culture, however, has made that sacred union something that is almost meaningless. When the white wedding dress once stood for purity, now, brides nowadays wear white just because that's what brides do. People live together and have babies together before marriage to see if they're "compatible" with each other. If it "all seems to work out," then maybe, just maybe, they get married. But then, if this "marriage thing" hits a tough spot, they just dump it and get divorced.

Marriage is non-negotiable. It is final. It is finished. It is "til death do us part." So, when you're dating, make sure God is in it. Make sure your path is right.

Your Valentine Is One Of Your Biggest Life Decisions. Don't Mess It Up!

This note came around Valentine's Day...

I love my valentine. I married the only valentine I ever had.

I *wanted* other valentines, especially when I was in high school, but I'm glad I never got any of them. God had just the right one, just for me.

If I had MY way, I would have dated around, messed around, had me some fun in high school. It might have been fun back then—for a season, as the Bible says—but what about now?

Instant pleasures last only as long as the pleasure lasts. Then, all you have left is guilt (or suppressed guilt).

When you do things God's way—wait on God, follow His leading, choose a spouse wisely—you *not only* get the instant pleasure, but you *also* get lifetime pleasure. Lifetime blessings. Lifetime non-guilt, in this area.

The Christian life is NOT about following a "list of rules" that the Bible lays out for all the "Christian peons." God's not the confused "man upstairs" that He is sometimes viewed as.

God has designed the Christian life for your good. When you make wise choices—even about who your valentine will be— God leads your life down a wonderful path.

Choose wisely, not emotionally. If you're on the "single" path at this stage of life, that is probably a good thing. God wants better for you, later.

I love my valentine, Mrs. Jamie, and I want ALL of you to be able to experience the lifetime pleasure that I'm talking about, too.

Psm. 62:5

Christian Living

The Christian life only begins at salvation. Each day is a new struggle. A new opportunity. A new battleground. A new anointing of God's mercy.

We have to stay alert every minute in order to not fall prey to the devil's traps. They're everywhere!

What's In It For Me?

Most people approach life with a "What's in it for me?" attitude.

That's not necessarily bad. It's just the way it is. Most of what you buy is to make your life better. Most of what you sell or give is to somehow make your life better. Most of what you think about is yourself.

Christianity is counter-cultural, though. It is basically the opposite of the "What's in it for me?" attitude. At least, that's how it appears.

Christianity is all about others. It should be, at least. At the heart of Christianity is loving God so much that it overflows into a genuine love for everyone around us—causing us to think less of ourselves.

But IS there anything in it for me? IS it really all about others?

There's PLENTY in it for you! Psalm 68:19 "Blessed be the Lord, who **daily loadeth us with benefits**, even the God of our salvation. Selah."

Selah just means, "Stop. Think about that while."

God promises joy and fulfillment in life. God promises blessings. God promises good feelings. God promises happy marriages. God promises sane and safe homes. God promises...

GOOD.

But wait... the world promises all those things too—fun, joy, happiness, a good time, fun marriages, good stuff...

So who's right? Who should you believe? They both promise the same thing!

Look at the history of each. Look back in time. Look at those who have lived by God's principles and compare them to those who have lived by worldly principles.

Which one delivers?

Only God can deliver on the promises. The devil just ends up a liar. As always.

Don't live in the moment. Sin promises a lot of pleasure in the moment. What's in it for you? If you serve God, what's in it for you? How about all of God's promises. That's what.

But it's so hard! you think.

I know. I agree. But it's worth it. At least in my life it has been. I'm praying for you to make it. At times I wonder if I want God's best for you even more than *you* want what's best for you.

I love you, class, and I pray for you. I prayed for you this morning, each by name. Love God. Love others. Do right.

Revived? Er... Normal

This note followed a revival service with Evangelist Billy Ingram.

Are you revived today?

Or should I ask it this way: are you normal today?

Revival Christianity is nothing extreme or abnormal. It's supposed to be how we live every day. It's not just for the super-intense Christians. It's not just for the most dedicated people.

It's for you.

Are you revived? Did you come this morning prepared to meet

with God? Seeking God? Willing to DO whatever He wants you to do?

Did you prepare your heart this morning? Like Bro. Ingram said several times last week... if you're coming to church prepared to worship, you'll be energized and ready. When people ask, "How are you?" your first response won't be, "Tired."

If you're always tired, that is a bad sign. It's a sign of spiritual weakness. Not that being *tired* is bad, but always coming to church lethargic and out-of-it is. It means you haven't come ready to worship God. It means you won't *get* much out of the service, and you won't *give* much through worship.

So I ask again... are you normal today? The only alternative is spiritual weakness. Maybe even disobedience!

Weeks like last week are crucial in your life. I hope it was a help to you.

Keep Up the Struggle [Story]

I love camp games.

Correction... I love *watching* camp games. I love taking pictures and video. Especially when clumsy people [Lexi again!] are involved.

This year, at camp, they played a giant version of steal the bacon, only the "bacon" was a giant 4-way tug-of-war rope. Every camper had a number from 1-5, and when they called a number, everyone (boys and girls separate) with that number rushed in to pull.

And pull, and pull and pull.

The camp staff *tried* to make the teams as even as possible, but it was useless. The Red Team girls were dominant. And the Blue Team guys were dominant. Every time.

When the Red Team girls came out, it was all over for the Blue Team. I mean... these girls were monsters. They foamed at the mouth, they snarled, and they looked downright mean—like they wanted to eat the scrawny little Blue Girls.

The Red Girls came off their line like Orcs, snarling and spitting, hair flying every direction.

They would grab hold of the rope (or the Blue Girls' hair), and would pull like maniacs. The Maniac of Gadera—you know the guy that lived in the tombs and could not be bound with ropes— would not have stood a chance against even one of these Red Girls, let alone a whole team of them. They were somehow super-human. Or, more likely, *non*-human.

Lexi, sadly, was not a Red Girl. She was a Blue Girl.

She had her little blue bandana strapped across her forehead, as if it would somehow help her demoralized companions. It seemed like every time Lexi's number got called she would rush out with eager anticipation, hope that this time would be different. Oh, maybe this time *she* would have some of that super-(or *non*)-human strength.

Nope.

She would face those maniacal Red Girls—those hissing, slashing, spitting and jeering Red Girls—she would pick up the rope, dig in her heels, throw her head back with all her might, let out a mighty war-whoop that would make any Samoan warrior proud, and pull with all her might.

Her grip was so tight that when she latched onto the rope, it was as if she could not let go. It was like when a kitten's claws get stuck in your shirt, and they cannot get out.

Heels dug in or not, she would inevitably fail.

I mean fail hard.

The rope—with her kitten claws and body attached—would lunge her forward, so that her face would smack right into the grass and skid across the surface.

But she was relentless. Her little kitten claws never let go. She would get dragged across the finish line over and over again. Each time it happened, she got more and more grass and mud stains across her front, so that when she stood up it looked as if the front half of her shirt and pants were a brownish-green color.

What I appreciated most was the struggle.

Good vs. Evil. An epic, timeless battle illustrated in these two teams: Red vs. Blue.

The struggle between Good and Evil is a daily "Steal the Bacon" game in our hearts. But it is no game. It is a real-life struggle.

At least it should be.

If you are NOT struggling, struggle. If you are not struggling, it might mean that you 1) Gave up, or 2) Are about to be blindsided. Both are bad.

The Christian walk is about knowing God intimately, and letting Him be in control of your life. When HE can take over the struggle, He will get the victory. Stay in the struggle.

Your Testimony In High School Matters

Have you ever thought, "Eh, big deal. Who cares what I do in high school. I'll just 'grow out of it' like everyone says. I mean, look at _____. HE had a rough past, and NOW look how God is using Him. I don't care about living for God now."

If that's your attitude, consider these few high schoolers who are now in their 20s and 30s, serving God with nothing holding them back.

Ms. Sarah. Mrs. Jamie and I worked in the youth department in Stillwater, OK from 2008 – 2010. During that time, Ms. Sarah was one of "our" teens. She graduated about the time that we were leaving, she headed to Heartland, and now she's here on staff! If she had been a rebellious teen, we would *never* have considered her for church staff. But, we saw a special love for God in her that almost no other teen had. Was she perfect? She'll be the first to tell you a big, "Nope." Guess what... no one is perfect! But it's about your heart for God. That starts for you

RIGHT NOW! In jr. high and high school. It matters.

Chris Pattison. I was a senior in high school and Chris Pattison was a Freshman or Sophomore. We played football and basketball together. We had lunch breaks together. All the while we were in school together, Chris was a godly example of what a young man should be and do as a Christian. Now, he's one of our missionaries to the Philippines. His testimony in high school helped our church be able to support him.

Brian Pattison. Chris's older brother, Brian, was a year older than me, but we had a few classes together. Brian was a soul-winner and a wonderful guy—even in high school. About 5 years ago, Brian planted a church in Chino, about 45 minutes from here. Our church helped him because of his good testimony in high school. Bro. Brian is a great friend and a good Christian man, and it started with his good choices in high school.

Pat Cook. One of my favorite classmates was a man named Pat Cook. He was the star everything—football, basketball, preacher, singer, etc—but he wasn't cocky about it. He sincerely loved the Lord, even as a high schooler. We graduated high school in 2004 together, and his testimony influenced me to be *much* more for God than I was currently being. He and I went to different colleges, but now he is in Menifee, planting a good Baptist church, which our church helped in. His passion for God in high school is influencing our youth ministry today.

Adam Marrujo. The graduating class before mine—the 2003 class—had two men in it: Brian Pattison and Adam Marrujo. Adam was one of my favorite people in high school. He was a plodder—a worker. He was never the super-star in sports, but he was always a phenomenal performer because he worked very hard at it. He always made me laugh, and his spirit was contagious. Bro. Adam is now planting a church in Riverside, starting on Easter. If it's a guy I knew in high school, Pastor always asks me, "What about this guy? Is he for real? Is he serious? Is he balanced? Is he a good guy?" With all these guys, I've been able to respond, "Yes. For sure," and we've supported them. It started in high school.

Think a bad attitude is no big deal? It is. You have NO idea what your future will be like. Don't sabotage your future before it gets here.

On the other side, many—most—of you are setting yourself up for a *wonderful* future. You're making GOOD choices, and I love that. Keep it up. Again, you have NO idea where God will bring you in your future, so live right NOW. It is always worth it. I promise.

At least, that's what I've noticed in life, so far...

Salvation Is Life-Changing

I've been excited by the recent baptisms. That is awesome!

Baptism is a sign (outward) of a change that has taken place in the heart (inward). Baptism was a death sentence for some people in the past. If they publicly declared that they had become a Christian (by getting baptized), they would be killed. Whoa.

Salvation is a life-changing experience—not just an eternity-changing experience. Sure, being saved ensures that you will go to heaven when you die, but it should also create a change in your day-to-day lives as you work to live for God.

Salvation can never be lost, but you can get to the point where it doesn't affect you any more. It can get old. Boring. The Bible can feel like a rulebook.

Uh oh. Careful about that! If it EVER starts to feel like the Christian walk is a drudgery, you're doing something wrong! The Christian's life is a walk of peace. Joy. Love. All the fruit that results from walking in the Spirit is good stuff (Gal. 5: 22-23).

So, baptism is the first step of a spiritual life—trying to make decisions that feed your spirit (the part of you that is God-conscious). Before salvation, the human's spirit is dead. When a person is saved, God makes that spirit come alive, and the Holy

Spirit (God) communes with us through OUR spirit.

Too deep? Nah.

It's actually pretty simple. When you are saved, growing as a Christian is about learning how to make spiritual decisions.

Baptism is the first spiritual decision. It identifies you as a Christian. It shows others—not just church people—that you became a Christian. If you are (or were) embarrassed about getting baptized... why? If you wouldn't get baptized in front of your school, or your friends, or your extended family... why?

As Christians, work on learning how to make spiritual decisions. If you have never been baptized, learn from the ones who recently took that step. They weren't embarrassed. Are you?

Are You a Thermostat or Thermometer?

I have a thermostat on my wall at home. Last night, I was making fun of my wife for turning it way down. "So... I'm paying money to run the AC just so I can cover up with blankets?"

The **thermostat** on the wall in the TOF room is usually set to about 69 or 70. When the temperature rises or falls from that, the thermostat adjusts the AC or heater to change the temperature. Some of you don't like how cold it always is. Sorry about your hypothermia.

On the other hand, a **thermometer** (or thermo-meter, as I like to call it) tells you what the temperature is. You stick it in your mouth (the old school mercury kind) and count to 8,000 before it finally registers your temperature. Then, you can't even read the crazy thing. Nowadays, we point a laser at the kid's forehead and the laser gun speaks to you: "Your body temperature is: 99 degrees." Thank you, technology.

Spiritually, you are either a thermostat or a thermometer.

- Thermostat – you CHANGE the spiritual temperature

(either hotter or colder, better or worse).

- Thermometer – you REFLECT the spiritual temperature (you're "into it" when everyone else is; but cold when they are, too.)

Today, influence others to be more on fire for God.

Good Friends Are For More Than Just Hanging Out

I just talked to my best friend on the phone this morning.

My friend John Lande was the best man at my wedding and a buddy all through college. We met each other after he'd been saved about four months and I knew right away, "This guy's CRAZY!"

I like crazy people.

God worked so much in his life his freshman year of Bible college, and I could see in him a friend that I knew would last a long time. I had lots of spiritual growing up to do, but this guy didn't have a clue. At least I was raised in a Christian home and had a good foundation, but he was the type that didn't have ANY of that. When he went to college days as a senior in high school, he had a permed-out afro, and he's a lanky, 6'3" weird white guy! He cut his hair just before college and came just for fun.

When God worked on his heart through all the preaching and the influences around him, he began to make good choices and chose to grow in the Lord. He became a godly influence to ME, and I grew to desire the kind of passion for God that HE had!

Good friends do that for you. Normal friends are just kind of there to hang out... Good friends drive you to passionately seek Christ and know His Word.

What kind of friend are you? What kind of friends do you have?

Maybe your closest friends should be ones that DRIVE you to

know Christ more and more, and maybe you should wean yourself off the ones that don't do you much good.

I can't wait for you to meet my friend John Lande. He's now the Heartland Singles Director at Southwest Baptist Church in Oklahoma City, and he took Bro. Gaddis' place when Bro. Gaddis became pastor of the church. John Lande is preaching our 2013 Preaching Rally... hopefully he doesn't still perm his hair.

Fun Is What You Make It

Do spiritual things excite you?

Does anything excite you

If you're a boring fuddy-dud, nothing is exciting to you. Nothing's fun. Nothing's thrilling.

It's like some teens don't like to show that they know how to have a good time with anything. It's like laughing is a sign of weakness or childishness, to them. It's like they're better than everyone else, and everyone who's having fun is an idiot.

What's with those people?! Man! Downers!

I'm glad we know how to have a good time. I'm glad the Teens of Faith isn't full of a bunch of downers.

Fun is what you make it. Boring people get bored.

Let me say that again... or at least make you read it again: Fun is what you make it. Boring people get bored.

The downers in life suck the energy out of a room. They're depressing. They're sad. They don't contribute. They make things awkward... almost on purpose, it seems!

These are all symptoms of a bad attitude... NOT a personality type. Introverted people CAN have fun along with a crowd of people. Extroverted people feed off a crowd's energy and love being around people. Introverts would rather be left alone. I get that. I AM one of those!

But being introverted is not the same as being a downer. Being a downer is a result of a bad attitude... which you CAN control. Being an introvert is sort of hard-wired into your brain. You can change some things but not everything. Having a bad attitude is not part of "who you are." A bad attitude is just you being a jerk. Don't be that. Choose to not be a jerk. Choose to not have a bad attitude.

If you're an introvert, make sure you're not mislabeled as "arrogant, stuck up, a jerk, goody-two-shoes, aloof, doesn't care, or WEIRDO!" How? By pushing yourself outside your comfort level and choosing to teach yourself to have fun in all types of circumstances. Fun is what you make it.

Don't like youth activities? Fun is what you make it. Don't like camp? It's on you.

This IS spiritual. I'm not just rambling about personality types. If you can choose your attitude (you can!), choose to have a good attitude about ALL areas of life. Choose to be involved. Choose to not be a downer. Choose to encourage others. Choose to grow up.

"It's so hard! I live in an extrovert's world! They ALWAYS enjoy life and it seems like the youth ministry is all about catering to THEM—youth camp, youth activities, door-knocking, even CLASS each week is a gathering of... people! I can't handle it. I'm an introvert!"

You're just being selfish if you think like that. You're focusing too much on yourself.

How much more do we preach on personal devotions—a daily quiet time of reading and personal reflection. No one is around. It's quiet.

If you say, "daily quiet time of reading" to an extrovert, for some, it's like you're saying, "Daily ripping the skin off your eyelids and pouring in gravel." Introverts thrive off of quiet time and reading. Extroverts thrive off of other people. Each needs to find balance.

You are probably a mix of both introverted and extroverted

qualities. Life is give-and-take. In this case, we're pushing camp and youth activities heavy because they can help you spiritually, even if they don't exactly "fit" your comfort level. Make sense?

I Always Appreciate Volunteers

Poor guys. You know... the ones I choose during sermon illustrations?

They always get beat up or embarrassed or hit or something. Sorry.

Well, they're great guys. They sacrifice themselves for the good of the sermon. I like that. I appreciate.

I appreciate it so much... today I need another!

Don't worry. You have a chance to win $1 (which, depending on what volunteer role you play, you will NOT be able to win, sorry).

But are you willing to volunteer for the good of the sermon? If someone is helped spiritually today as a result of your involvement, that's a blessing that goes to *you* and *you* alone. Pretty cool!

So help me out today, will you?

Love you guys, especially you poor ~~saps~~ volunteers.

God Works Even When We Cannot See Him [Story]

Mrs. Schaffer called on me to answer the question. I hesitated.

"Stand up, Ryan."

I knew the answer; I just did not want to stand up. I had wet my pants.

I was a scrawny kid, and was wearing my oversized coat in my seat. I pulled it off my shoulders and hugged it around my waist

—you know... like I *always* wear my coats. I stood. Slowly.

The taller I got, the lower the jacket went, covering my navy blue school uniform slacks. I had a plan: hide 'til it dried.

Moments later, without the school bell ringing, a stroke of luck came my way... recess time. What a strange turn of events! In the nick of time, everyone was dismissed.

As I rose to exit, I heard my name. Gently. Softly.

My classmates wasted no time getting outdoors, hardly glancing my way, too excited about this impromptu break.

I glanced down at my pants, then up at the teacher. *Uh oh. I'm pegged. How could she tell? It blends right in!*

"Ryan, is there anything wrong?"

The rest is history, as they say. It ended up okay. My parents picked me up and I got the rest of the day off school. My classmates were never the wiser, and I returned the next day a new man.

I recently heard an atheist talking about her version of God—a loving grandpa-type of character, but one that would scorch you with lightning if you ever messed up. That's not God. That's not MY God. That's not THE God.

God is like Mrs. Schaffer. Loving. Caring. Gentle. Helpful.

As a kindergartener, I thought that recess was a stroke of luck. As I reflect on it now, it's obvious that the teacher saw my plight and stepped in to save the day—and save me from embarrassment, too.

God works behind the scenes, in ways we will never recognize until later. Stay faithful. You'll see Him in your life, even if you wet your pants.

Events

At certain events like Harold Camping's failed prophecies and the September 11 bombing anniversaries, we reflect on how those days might affect us.

Well... the World Didn't End

This note came after another failed "End of the World" prediction...

Just like all the other crazy predictions of the past, the world didn't end... again.

Too bad. I wanted to be in heaven right now. It's a lot better than this ol' earth!

But WHAT IF the world had ended last week, like some people predicted? WHAT IF the rapture had happened? WHAT IF God judged you?

That's what's going to happen some day. I'm not trying to scare you... it's just the truth! God will judge you based on His law. If you've broken it, you are unholy and have to pay for your sin.

Have you ever stolen? How about lied? Or *hated* someone? Jesus said hate is as bad as murder (same root), and you'll face God as a lying, murdering thief!

Rev. 21:8 But the fearful, and unbelieving, and the abominable, and murderers, and whoremongers, and sorcerers, and idolaters, and all liars, shall have their part in the lake which burneth with fire and brimstone: which is the second death.

1 Cor. 6:9-10 Know ye not that the unrighteous shall not inherit the kingdom of God? Be not deceived: neither fornicators, nor idolaters, nor adulterers, nor effeminate, nor abusers of themselves with mankind, 10Nor thieves, nor covetous, nor drunkards, nor revilers, nor extortioners, shall inherit the kingdom of God.

I'm not judging you, but God will.

So WHAT IF He had judged you last week? Would you have gone to heaven or hell?

Jesus paid the penalty for your sin and gave you the gift of salvation. All you have to do to receive that gift is repent of your sin and turn to Christ, giving him your life. HE gives you new life--new desires, passions, and impulses. He gives you the comfort of knowing Him. He gives you the assurance that you're in Him.

That's how I know the answer to the WHAT IF question, personally. WHAT IF God had come last week? I'd be okay. I'm saved by Jesus' blood. I was born again way back in Nov. 1991. I remember the time that I believed in my heart and spoke the words of trust to God in prayer. Rom. 10:9 *That if thou shalt confess with thy mouth the Lord Jesus, and shalt believe in thine heart that God hath raised him from the dead, thou shalt be saved.*

How about you? When did you do that?

Never? Then how about today?

This Day in History

This note came around 9/11...

I don't know how much they emphasize the terrorist bombings in your schools, but if you're old enough to remember some of the details of the 9/11 attacks, you know it was a huge deal to America. It unified us, and it sparked a war.

What happened that day was an outrage? We were attacked by Muslim terrorists who, for the most part, were not from the outside but from the inside. I hate traitors. I hate people who use our resources and live in our land and then spend all their time trying to destroy us or cut down our nation. I hate it when people from other countries come here to live, but the whole time they're here they talk about how much better their country is. If you like it so much, go back!

But this isn't a rant about being American. It's more of a rant about the lives that were taken, and the outrage that was shown following the attacks. Think about the thousands of people who died that day. Think about the shock of everyone else in the nation as they watched the towers collapse. Astounding.

Now... think back to another time when just as many people lost their lives, but lost them for a whole different reason. Have you ever read Foxe's Book of Martyrs or The Trail of Blood? These are books that detail some of the atrocities of the established churches (like the Catholics) back in the days when they had full power. Thousands of Bible-believers were killed because they would not bow to the false teachings or recant their faith.

Where was the outrage then?

What about the missionaries who come through our church and say that other countries all over the world hate Christians, and persecution of Christians is a real thing? Where's our outrage about people even today who are giving their lives for their faith?

God help us to be as spiritually driven to stand for truth as we Americans were to stand for our liberty.

Family

Almost my entire family is involved in our ministry. My wife and kids come everywhere with me, my dad is my pastor (and boss), my mom is the church custodian, my sister is our pianist, my older brother is a teacher and sound man, and my younger brother will eventually (hopefully) be moving back someday.

Family ties are tight, especially when you are all on the same page philosophically and spiritually. The following notes talk about family in some way.

My Dad and My Father

Happy Fathers Day.

Dads are cool. Dads can do anything. Dads are tough. My dad can beat up your dad... from the pulpit, that is.

Whether you have a great relationship with your dad or not, you need to thank God today for where he's put you in your life. I don't know where each of you are in your walk with God or in your relationship with your dad, but I can tell you this: you have a heavenly Father who loves you even more than your dad does.

That's cool.

My dad's pretty tough. But my Father can beat up my dad. Know what I mean? My heavenly Father is way bigger than all my problems or fears or worries. He's on my side.

Dad loves me, but my Father loves me more. My Father loves me so much that he sent His Son to die for me. Dad never sent my brother to die for me (sometimes I wish he would have!) My Father has tons of mansions. Dad just has a trailer he converted to a house. My Father has streets of gold. Dad lives on a dirt road with potholes. My dad's a preacher, but he's not original... he just repeats what my Father said first.

So anyway, Dad's great, and I thank God for him. Every time I'm up at 3am with Abe, I thank God for my dad. While my life has been great with my dad, some of you might not have been able to experience a dad like that. Hey, you'll live 70ish years here. You'll spend eternity with your Father.

How Dare You Miss Church Last Sunday

This was the note we gave the week after our son was born...

Oh wait... WE missed church last Sunday.

But for good reason. I was working hard to deliver you a new class mascot, remember? Oh yeah, and Mrs. Jamie did some work too. (She's going to kill me for that comment.)

We're proud to present to you Abraham Wyatt Rench.

Thank you for praying for my wife. It means a LOT to have you all around for our first kid. I can't wait to see how God stretches me as a parent, and I hope that spiritual stretching ends up being helpful to YOU in some way. The way I see it, I'll be learning a lot of spiritual truths through parenting, and many of those same truths will transfer to youth ministry.

Plus, babies do dumb and funny stuff all the time, so I'll have some illustrations built right in!

I sure love you all and hope you have as great a family of your own someday as I have now! It's all your choice... so guys, choose a godly lady. Ladies, choose a godly man! Can't go wrong when He's first, and Abe is just another reminder of that in OUR lives.

This Is My MAIN Ministry In Church

Have you ever stopped and thought about your life?

What kind of relationships do you have? What kind of friends do you have? How important is your family to you? How important are your friends?

My ministries here at Calvary Baptist Church include several areas: youth, music, and whatever else.

But what's my main ministry? Is it youth? I spend most of my time there. Maybe that's it. Is it music? It's an essential part of the worship of God each week, and it could be argued that godly music is more important than a youth ministry. Is my main ministry as an associate pastor—trying to support our pastor in all the areas of ministry I can?

Actually, my main ministry is none of those things. Before I'm a youth pastor, before I'm a music director, before I'm a church staff member, God has given me other roles. Or, other ministries, you could say.

My main role is to be a Christian. That's a given. My relationship with the Lord comes first, but right on the heels of being a godly man I am called to be a godly husband and father.

God ordained the family unit, and it has been around even before the church. That doesn't necessarily make it more important to God than the church, but it shows us that God's way is timeless. Family is important to God.

Children are given to parents, not a church. Families are tight little "ministries" in themselves.

You know what my main ministry is now? For the next couple decades, my main ministry will be to lead my family to love the Lord. With Charlotte being born this week, my "ministry" just expanded!

Youth groups come and go. You will come and go. Your friends will come and go. You know what? Your family and my family will always be families. You can't change that. So, I had absolutely better be sure that I invest in the one place that is closest to me—my family.

I Keep My Kids Involved In Ministry On

Purpose — For You

This was written around my son's third birthday...

Abe is three. Just in case you were wondering.

Oh, you weren't? What jerks!

You know, my prayer as a youth pastor/dad has been that I can show you through my family's example that ministry can be incredibly fun! I want you to know that serving God is the BEST thing a family can do together.

We've been at it with kids for three years now. It's been quite a journey. Abe and Charlotte have taught ME a lot about what it means to be a Christian. They have challenged me to be a better Christian and work to be an example as a dad.

I purposely tell stories of my kids and have them around youth activities because I want to show you that families are not a burden to life—they're a blessing! I've met people who pretty much check out of life while they are raising their kids. I am all for devoting time to them, but not at the expense of the greater ministry: the church.

Too much of anything is bad. Too much family (if you are not a connected church member) is bad. Too much church (if you are neglecting your family) is bad. Is it possible to have both, and do well at both?

Yes. YES! It is possible. God has called me to preach. He has also called me to be a dad, and a husband, and a teacher, and... He has called me to a lot of things.

If God calls, He will also enable.

Faithful is he that calleth you, who also will do it. 1 Thes. 5:24.

If God has called me to do all these things, HE is going to have to be the one to do the work. He gives us plenty of time to do all the things He has called us to do. Don't waste His time that He has given you, and do ALL to His glory!

Reflecting On Christmas Traditions

This note was from the day after Christmas...

What did you do yesterday?

We opened Santa's gifts in our stockings, opened our cool gifts and headed up to my parents' for breakfast, more presents, lunch and play-time. While we were waiting, Garret opened one of his presents early—a rocket—so the brothers and nephews put it all together and shot it off a few times. Man-time to the extreme. It got caught in a neighbor's tree the first time, got lost behind the Bailey's house the second time and the last time we finally dialed it in and landed it pretty close to us.

Talk about extreme man-time... in the field where we were shooting off the rocket was a bunch of golf balls. We gathered them all up and started hitting them back in the field. When Nathan went out to get some of the balls that didn't go so far, Pastor started blasting as many golf balls as he could hit right at Nathan's head. The war was on. Nathan started hitting them back at us and it turned into many near-death experiences. Pastor's ankle was the only casualty.

After golf we played some more inside games, ate some leftovers and hung out as a family. Christmas is an awesome time to be around the people that you love. It's not all about the gifts. I hope and pray that all of you work to build strong families some day. I pray that no matter what your upbringing is like right now, you choose to please God with your life and watch Him do amazing things with your future. God's blessings are amazing, and I'm reminded often of the blessings of lifetime faithfulness. Not MY faithfulness but my parents—people who have been faithful for a lifetime and are reaping amazing blessings from God through their family today.

Only Happy Moms Are Allowed In Church Today

Wait... does "Happy Mother's Day" mean that only happy

moms are allowed in church today? I say yes. If they're cranky... kick them out. This is happy mother's day.

I love my mom. I wouldn't be where I am today without my mom (oldest Mothers Day joke ever.)

I also love my wife. She's the coolest mom ever. When I married my wife, I had no idea she'd be as good of a mom as she is. I don't think SHE knew she'd be such a good mom. There's no mom college to teach girls how to be good moms. Somehow, my wife is doing it right.

You'd better respect these young moms, man! They're tough! My wife has been up every night for the past 2 months feeding that baby at crazy times. Just last night she was up at 10:30 and then again at 3:30. And that's a LONG stretch of time for that baby to sleep! Mrs. Jamie is happy with 5-hour stretches of sleep. I'm telling you... being a mom isn't for wimps.

That's on top of caring for all you snotty nosed little whiners, too. Momma Jamie has continued in choir, all her churchy duties, camp registrations... everything. She's a champ! Some of you boys (not men) get the sniffles and you're out of commission. Poor things. Maybe my wife can teach you how to toughen up (that's embarrassing.)

Not only is Mrs. Jamie cool, but Mrs. Gina and Mrs. Lori are pretty awesome, also. I mean... Mrs. Gina has had a ton of major surgeries and she looks and acts like nothing's even wrong! She's got more metal in her than a transformer! She is cool! And Mrs. Lori... don't even mess with her! She's the mother of Evan... enough said. Pray for Mrs. Lori! She's got a son who wants to sing and dance instead of pillage and plunder! *sigh. Also, I bet none of you girls can beat her on the raft at Ironwood.

Moms are awesome. Love your mom and she'll be your biggest cheerleader in life. Fact.

Mamamama

Charlotte's first and favorite word is *mamamamama*...

I'm okay with that. She's working on dadadada.

There's just something about moms, right? When I put Charlotte down, nothing happens. She's like, *All right, done with dad. On to my toys.*

But when MOM puts her down it's a different story. Dramatic rageful tears of rejection, here we come! *MOM! Don't leave me! How could you put me down? Don't you LOVE me? Don't you WANT to carry me around all the day?! Why are you doing this to me? I can't bear it! WAAAA!...*

That's about how it goes. Charlotte loves her Mommy. And she's got a good one.

Abe has grown out of that particular clingy phase, but he still loves his Mommy like crazy. His phase now is fits of clench-jawed wrestle-mania! His form of love wrestling mom less. He has all this energy (rage?) pent up inside him, and he goes to release it in a psycho burst of fury. When he does that, sometimes Mom is the only one around to receive his outburst. Poor Mrs. Jamie. But then something clicks in his mind, and he thinks, *Oh, wait... spankings hurt... I don't hit girls. Mommy's a girl. I love my mom. I'd better chill.*

Yeah, you'd better! Nobody punches *my* wife. Especially not some punk 2-year old!

But Abe loves his mom, so he stops short of the full fury he was about to release. He relaxes his jaw. He loosens his clenched fists. He lets out a calming sign. Aahhh. That's better.

It's kind of sad when you show love by NOT showing as much rage. Good one, Abe. Well, it's something, I guess. Happy Mother's Day, Mrs. Jamie (and all other moms who might be reading this)!

"Just Because, Dad"

"Come on, kiddos. Hurry up and get dressed for bed." I was sitting on the floor, arm resting on Abe's toddler bed, back against the dresser, waiting to read their bedtime story *Prince Caspian.* "You're taking too long."

Abe finished dressing, ran out to use the restroom, came back into the room and squeezed me around the neck and shoulders, giving me a man-sized hug. "I love you so much, Dad."

"Thanks, my man! Why'd you say that?" I said.

He thought a minute. "I don't know."

"Just because?" I said.

"Yeah. Just cuz."

I'll take it. Any time.

Missions

Every January is our church's missions emphasis month. These notes encourage teens to surrender to church planting and foreign missions.

Young Men Need a Burden For California

This note followed a church planter's sermon on the need for California church planting. Since this note, three other church plants have started in this area, praise God...

If you were here last week you heard one of the best presentations on church planting ever.

We are intentional about keeping home missions in front of you because of the very reasons that Bro. Irmler gave. If no one is planting churches here in America, eventually there will be no one to support foreign missions.

Whenever I am in Oklahoma (like I am tonight giving away our TOF Home Missions Offering) for the Church Planting Conference, I am always very careful about where our money goes. Of course, EVERYWHERE in America needs the gospel, but if you have never been out of California, you may not have seen how many churches are in places like Nebraska, Oklahoma, Texas and other places in the Midwest. My wife's church is a strong, independent, Fundamental, KJV, soul-winning Baptist church in Indianapolis—just like our church. The difference in Indiana is that there are dozens more churches just like ours within a 30 minute drive of her home church! She lived a while in a town of 20,000, and there were at least 5 Baptist churches there.

Here... not even close. Faith Baptist Church is 15 miles up the road in Wildomar, and they're pretty much the only other one here in the whole Temecula Valley that uses the King James Bible! In Temecula, Murrieta, Winchester and the surrounding communities there are probably about 300,000 people. And two Baptist churches. (There's another small Southern Baptist church down by Pechanga, but that's it).

California needs more churches! Bro. David Hetzer is 40 minutes south in San Marcos, Bro. Christenson is 30 minutes away in Fallbrook, Bro. Beard and Bro. Leavell are in the Hemet area, there are a couple Baptist churches in Corona, a couple in Escondido... I'm naming HUGE communities with tens of thousands of people and we can only come up with about 1 or 2 churches per city.

Every time we're at the conference, Pastor and I always try to give our money to places like Seattle, Minnesota, anywhere in California, Florida, New Orleans, Nevada, Arizona and such— anywhere there are not already tons of churches. We're not judging the church planters that go to other places like Springfield, MO or Oklahoma City, but no one can argue the point that the need is greater in CA than it is in Oklahoma City. Maybe someone will have to drive an extra 6 minutes in order to get to a good church in Oklahoma, but it's just my opinion that they can manage. I digress, and I am being a little facetious now. ☺ But the point is still the same—our TOF Home Missions Fund will primarily be spent where we perceive the need is greatest. You can count on that.

I can't wait to see you Sunday to report on how it's going this week!

Missions – God's Heartbeat

Someone once said that missions is the heartbeat of God.

God cares for every single person on this earth. From the most remote Alaskan village to the most densely populated metro, God cares for everyone.

So who's going to get out of their comfort zone and go reach lost souls across the world? Praise God for those of you who have surrendered your life to God. You've basically said, "God, use me wherever you want me."

What if He calls you to Alaska? Will you go? Are you that surrendered? Tomorrow's Alaska Missions Trip is a time to simply be exposed to people who have it harder than us. Do you care for souls enough to go?

"Why, yes! I want to be a missionary some day." Okay. Are you being a missionary right now?

That's where it hurts. Anyone can be a missionary "someday." What about now?

And... whether you're called to be a missionary or not... are you giving? That's something that ALL of us can and should do. Do you regularly give to missions by faith? "I don't have any money." I said by faith. Not by you having money.

God will bless your faith if you have it. Missions is a great "litmus test" to see if you have real faith. On a scale of 1-10, how passionate are you about missions?

I Explained the Missions Trip To the Guys This Way

This summer, we are taking a group to LA to visit some church plants. On Wednesdays, as you know, we are working through our BIBS book to allow you to qualify for this trip.

When I was talking to the guys about it on Wednesday, something interesting came to mind. I told them that doing your daily BIBS (daily Bible reading devotional book) is NOT about being a perfect Christian. It's not even about being a GOOD Christian. It's not about becoming a Christian, or staying a Christian, or anything like that.

I told them that I don't expect daily Bible reading to make you a perfect person. That's not the goal. The goal isn't necessarily that YOU change. Change can be forced. Change can be faked. Change can be outward.

The MAIN reason for doing daily devotions is because it feeds the spirit. The missions trip is a spiritual trip. It's a missions trip. It's a ministry trip. It's not a vacation, a sight-seeing time, or a trip just for fun. It's a missions ministry trip. We want to 1) help our church planters, and 2) expose you to inner city church planting. If we're taking a group of people on a spiritual missions trip, I'd prefer to take spiritual people.

Does that mean you walk around talking about spiritual things all day? Like God and the Bible? Maybe. Actually... no.

Being "spiritual" just means that you feed your spirit. You try to live by the Spirit. That's it. Feed your spirit, and you are "spiritual." Read your Bible and pray—and you'll be feeding your spirit. A spiritual missions trip is about spiritual people doing spiritual work. So don't expect that two weeks of daily Bible reading with radically transform you into some weirdo who goes around talking about the Greek definition of whatever...

Just be a normal person. But be a spiritual normal person.

Thankfulness

Unexpressed gratitude is ingratitude.

If you didn't say, "Thank you," you are not thankful.

We all know we SHOULD be thankful, but we forget. Sometimes it takes a gentle reminder note to encourage us to express the gratitude in our hearts.

Be a Thanker To Turn Thankees Into Other Thankers

This note came after a church member donated scores of personalized notebooks and notepads to our teens...

Be specifically thankful...or it's not thankfulness.

After receiving their Teens of Faith notebooks (donated by Mary Wright), Lexi and Keli asked Mrs. Rench to point out Mrs. Wright to them. With notebooks in hand and a smile on their faces, they introduced themselves and thanked Mrs. Wright for donating all the books and print materials for the Be Our Guest outreach.

You should have seen Mary's face after they thanked her... priceless.

In fact, Mary practically yelled at me afterwards... "Bro. Ryan, you'd better stop telling your kids to come up and thank me... they're making me CRY too much!!" ☺ I'm not telling you to stop... keep it up!

SHE was thankful that YOU were thankful. Isn't that a cool cycle? One person does something nice, is thanked, wants to do more, the "thanker" feels good that the "thankee" liked the thanks, and thanks others, and those "thankees" like to be thanked, so they become "thankers" of others... You get the point.

Be thankful. Be specifically thankful.

"God, thank you for loving me." Sure, that's good... but how about, "God, even though I was a lying, blaspheming, adulterous thief, thank you for STILL sending your Son to die for me and take my sins away when I accepted Him as my Savior."

Don't be too general; be specific and write it down. Don't write, "Be thankful," write:

- Ask Bro. Ryan or Bro. Ken to point out Mary Wright
- Thank Mary Wright for the notebooks.
- Write mom and dad a thank-you note.

You're a blessing to us and we thank God for you basically every day. I really mean that.

Are You Being Intentionally Thankful?

This note followed a special Thanksgiving testimony service we had at our church...

I pray you had a great Thanksgiving break.

I know you all can't wait to get back to school, but there's only one more day! (Oh don't remind me, Bro. Ryan! Why do you gotta be like that?!) Sorry. It's part of my job.

Were you thankful this week? Last Sunday night it was like we ran out of time because SO many people had SO much to be thankful for! What a blessing it was to hear so many of you speaking up, and we thank God for you.

"I'm Thankful For... the BIBLE!"

I liked Keli's testimony at the Praise and Pie night a couple weeks ago: "I'm thankful for... the BIBLE!" That's it. I love that.

Is that your heart?

I hope so. That's what the whole Bible Study series is about. Learning to hear what God said and, through that, what He is saying through His Word. You HAVE to get this. You HAVE to learn and know your Bibles. If you don't, who will? If you think you'll make it in life any other way, what way is that?!

Love God, love others, do right.

Never Have a "Gimme-Gimme" Spirit

With the fundraisers we do with our church, I hope you never develop a "gimme-gimme" spirit. Our church people sacrifice a lot. Please don't think that everything should be given to you. Rather, look for ways to give to others! That's the fun part!

Obedience always brings blessing. So obey God.

Someone who recognizes that all blessings come from God should automatically be grateful for what he's received! So, first give of God's abundance to you (time, energy, talent...), AND be grateful for everything he continues to bless you with. That cycle can't be beat... it's Bible!

Do right.

Be Expressively Thankful For the $1900 and Counting

This note followed our annual yard sale fundraiser...

We couldn't have had a successful yard sale without Mrs. Jamie or Mrs. Rench. They are amazing ladies who've poured hours into preparing this whole fundraiser for you.

You'll never know the amount of work that is done behind the scenes of anything until you do it. It's like the stage crew of a play. When you're watching the play you don't think about the teams of people in the background getting the props, or the person who printed the tickets, or the administrator who scheduled the theater, or the janitor who cleaned the floors and bathrooms... you get the idea.

Be over-the-top thankful for everything that comes your way. "Well, I worked for this money. I deserve my cut. You're supposed to do these fundraisers for me to be able to go to camp."

Actually, that's not true. No one deserves anything, and we don't have to do fundraisers for camp. It's a privilege of our church, and you'd do well to be over-the-top thankful. You should have that kind of gratitude for a lot of things. Learn to be expressive and specific.

So anyway, congrats on the great fundraiser. If you have a voice left after shouting at every car passing by, you're awesome.

Think Thankfulness This Thursday. Thanks.

Did you read the Baptist Times article on thankfulness yet? Bro. Hardy made a great point in the article in saying that the 9 lepers who were healed by Jesus didn't finish the job. Jesus healed 10 lepers that day, and only one returned to thank Jesus. It seems like Jesus expected the other lepers to complete the circle and return to Jesus to thank him for healing them. When they didn't, Jesus took it as a time to teach a lesson on gratitude.

I hope that in this season especially, you are the most grateful person in the world. I hope you take it on yourself to express your gratitude for others, for family, for things, for gifts, for everything. God has blessed you with so much. Thanksgiving is a holiday set up for being thankful, but we should always be thankful people. The Thanksgiving spirit should carry over into this season of giving, too.

Are you thankful? Think about how you've expressed gratitude lately. Be purposely and genuinely thankful, and let is show. Express it. Show it. Write it. Say it. Then say it again. Don't be flippant. Be sincere. Be direct. Be heard. Don't let someone else be thankful for you. YOU be thankful.

Your parents pay a lot of money for you to be alive and healthy. The Myers family was super gracious to allow us to crash their house on Friday. Pastor has poured his life into this church. The Bakers give rides, provide money, and donate a lot of their time to you, despite Bro. Ken being 86 years old (you had to be here last week). ☺

You are surrounded by people that constantly give to you. I'm writing this to myself! When I look at it that way, I'm a horrible person! I should be WAY better at thanking people for what they do. How about you?

Five Ways To BE Thankful (Hint: Its not Just SAYING "Thanks.")

Being thankful is more than *saying* "Thank you."

Anyone can write a thank-you note (although few people do!). Anyone can say a quick, "Thanks." Anyone can say or write the words "Thank you."

But *are* you a thankful person?

Pastor has been asking us that in the preaching recently, hasn't he? He's been pointing out to us that we are to BE thankful, not just GIVE thanks.

This changes everything! We can no longer get away with just a simple little "thanks" every now and then. In order to BE a thankful person, you should put on the mindset of a thankful person.

Here are a few thoughts on BEING thankful.

1.   **Express thanks to God.** Spend time *every day* thanking God for what you have. Are you saved? You

mean... you won't spend eternity in hell? You mean... you get to have a relation with the eternal, immortal, invisible, only wise God?! Wow! No matter how bad you think your life is, the worst life on earth is still better than 60 seconds in hell. Thank God for that.

2. **SAY "Thank you."** Obviously, BEING a thankful person is more than just saying "Thank you." But it DOES include saying it! Get in the habit of being thankful by saying, "Thank you" to others.

3. **Write "Thank you" notes.** Whenever someone does something kind for you, write them a note. This includes but is not limited to birthday gifts, people taking you out to eat, when someone is a blessing to you, etc. Hand-written notes are a novelty these days. Try them out!

4. **Think throughout your day.** On Monday I caught myself thinking of Pastor's sermon and all the little things that happen in my life. I'm thankful for small things like my mom helping out all the little grandkids, or feeding us Mac N Cheese and hot dogs for dinner. I'm thankful for that kind of stuff when I *think* about it.

5. **When you remember that you forgot to be thankful, make it right.** We took a few of you out to Cici's the other day after door-knocking. We love spending the time with you and it's thanks enough for us to watch you grow in the Lord, serving Him at door-knocking. But Matthew McCreary, the next day in Sunday school, came up to me and said, "Thank you for that meal yesterday. I really appreciated it! I think I thanked you for the ride home, but I couldn't remember if I'd thanked you for the lunch, too. So, thank you!" To be honest, I can't remember if he thanked us on Saturday or not. I thought it was awesome, though, that he came back later and thanked us—just in case!

A thankful person does more than just say, "Thanks," every now and then. He or she IS thankful—like, as a *character* trait.

Are you a thankful person?

Being Thankful Is More Than Being Courteous

Are you a thankful person?

What have you intentionally thanked someone for, recently?

A couple weeks ago, I gave about 25 books away. They cost me about $5 each. The cost doesn't matter so much to me as the response. What was somewhat surprising was how few people sincerely thanked me for them.

Sure, most of the people (teens and adults) were *courteous*, but few were specifically *grateful*. I think they all said, "Thank you" or "Thanks," because that's the polite thing to do, but there's a different tone when people are *thankful*.

Thankful people aren't owed anything. Don't get in a rut where you're always *owed* an activity, or a ride, or a good sermon, or a meal, or a book, or a house, or a loving parent, or health, or... anything. No one owes you anything. Thankful people know this. When they get something—anything—they're grateful. And it shows.

Thankful people are expressively specific. When you're thankful, be sure to express it in specific terms. At the end of the book day, a few hours later, only one or two of them *specifically* thanked me for the gift. About half of them thanked me in passing on their way out the door as a general courtesy, but only a couple people were expressly grateful for the gift. Gratefulness shows in words, eye contact, excitement, body language... everything! "Thank you VERY much for this book! I really appreciate it. I know it wasn't free! I promise I'll be using it, and thank you for giving us the choice..." You get the idea.

Thankful people are intentional. It takes work to be thankful. Jesus' gift of healing to the 10 lepers was unconditional, but for 9 of them, it was a little bit incomplete. The one leper who returned to thank Jesus was the one Jesus highlighted. The other 9 lepers were probably grateful in their hearts, but they weren't intentional about returning to express it, so they got painted in a bad light (for eternity!) Be intentional about thanking God and others for blessings.

Thankfully Dedicated. [Short Story]

James was a scrawny puke, and hated getting caught.

He cut the cattle fences on Coach McGuire's ranch to get back at him for making him run extra laps in basketball practice—29 laps, to be exact. He got caught and sentenced to 25 hours of community service—on Coach's ranch.

Working with Coach, though, wasn't as bad as James thought it would be.

After 4 days of working together, Coach told James, "I believe in you, kid. I think you have what it takes to be in the NBA."

James' chest swelled with inspiration at Coach McGuire's words. Never had anyone told him that—not since his dad died three years earlier, anyway. Since then, James had been trouble. To everyone.

But hearing Coach's words and spending time working on his ranch, James went on to become the hardest worker on the basketball team. His teammates were shocked. He ran hard on every drill, ran hard on every lap, and ran hard in every game. He practiced early and stayed late, working on his fundamentals. Coach said he could make it to the NBA.

James' sophomore year, he won the "Most Improved" award. He was a starting player his Junior year, but broke his arm midway through the season. Coach told him, "You'll be all right. Push through and you'll be back on the court next year." James' Senior year was his best year ever. He went on to play in college and was drafted to the NBA a year later, just like Coach had said.

James took Rookie of the Year, and acknowledged his high school coach on the podium. Later, after winning an Olympics gold medal for Team USA, he scribbled a note, boxed up the medal, wrote an address on the label and shipped it to a little ranch in Nevada.

The address said, "Coach McGuire," and the note simply said, "Thanks, Coach. You're like a dad to me. More than just *saying* 'thanks,' though, I want you to have this. It's all because of you that I'm here. Thankfully dedicated. –James." *(p.s. not a true story)*

Giving

Teens are church members too.

Therefore, teens should be givers. Tithing is the responsibility of every church member, and NOT tithing is the same as pulling money out of the offering plate when it goes by—robbery!

Beyond the tithe, I think teens should give to missions, to building funds, and to every special offering they can. I always had a LOT of money in high school, and I sincerely think it was because my parents taught me to give.

I want the same for my teens, too, as you will see through these notes...

It Seems Weird, But Giving Blesses YOU

I almost feet carnal, but if you really dive into the study yourself and think of just the word *abound*, you'll find that God wants to give you so much that it's spilling over! What a cool principle! I want to get in on that cycle. 2 Cor. 9:8-13:

1. God abundantly blesses. (abundance, enriched)

2. Our hearts our filled with gratitude and generosity. (thanksgiving, bountifulness)

3. We desire to give to others. (bountifulness, administration, ministration, liberal distribution)

4. God and the gospel are glorified.

5. The cycle starts all over again.

It starts with knowing everything you have is already God's, and he LETS us be blessed in this way. You show me a joyful person and I'll show you a giving person (2 Cor. 8:2). This Sunday, lets all purpose to know God's will and get in on that cycle.

I hope you've spent the week asking for God's leading and help. If you live your life in faith, you can't go wrong according to the Bible!

Love God. Love others. Do right.

The Goal Of Giving Is Involvement; Not An Amount

This note came the week after we hit our offering goal...

Did you notice the thermometer on Sunday?

We made our goal!

But, like I've said a few times before, the REAL goal isn't the money amount we're shooting for... the REAL goal is involvement. If we could have everyone involved in some way in the Teens of Faith Home Missions Fund, God would blow that thermometer out of the water! If every member really sought God on how he or she could be involved, and really made it a spiritual discipline to be involved every week, we'd see God bless in ways you can't imagine.

He promised He would. And remember from Sunday... He's good for EVERY promise He makes, no matter what. So why not bank on that promise? The promise to "give and it shall be given unto you." Get in on the cycle!

Mrs. Jamie, Pastor and I are going out to Heartland Baptist Bible College in January to give our Home Missions Fund to church planters all over America. It's such a privilege to be involved, and we might be the only youth group there who's done that... I don't remember (from when I was a student) any other youth group bringing offerings to the conference.

Giving is a privilege. I hope you never get cynical about the pastor or the Bible when you hear or read something about giving. Non-givers are cynics. Givers are blessed and happy, and can't give enough! Be a giver... for YOUR sake!

We sure love you and we're glad you're here tonight. Do right.

Your Giving Blessed Others

Our thermometer each week showed your progress from the weekly offerings, and just last week we gave it all away!

Guess what? Through YOUR giving and YOUR testimony, OTHER churches will be doing the same. Bro. Davison mentioned from the pulpit that we were taking weekly offerings, and I had a few pastors tell me later, "That's a great idea! I want to do that!" Praise God!

You can read the Thermometer for all the ministries we were able to help. It was SUCH a blessing to be able to stand up and say "$50" for 12 different church plants all over the country.

You can't understand our passion for the Church Planting Conference unless you're there to experience it first hand, and I want SO badly for you all to be able to make it there some day! I know it's an expensive and short trip, but if you can save up and make it out there some day, it could literally be life changing. I'm not interested in people's "life-changing" books or videos... I'm talking about God calling some of you men to preach under ministries like this, or burdening you for churches all over. That's the kind of lasting life changes I'm interested in.

Like we've preached on Wednesdays: others are blessed when you serve the Lord. This week was another perfect example of that Bible truth. Do right!

You Gave $1k At the Church Planting Conference

This note came after donated our annual offerings to church planters...

Our youth group was able to be a great testimony to a lot of people last week.

When I was at the Church Planting Conference at Heartland, we gave away our offerings of $1000. Praise God! We were able to help several church planters across America.

One of the coolest things was that *last year* we inspired other youth groups to bring offerings, so *this year* we were not the only youth group represented. Praise God for your sacrifice and faithfulness all year. That's the goal of giving. Learn now that you need to give sacrificially and faithfully, and God will bless you more and more over your life.

Think Our Class Will Give the MOST To Missions? That's Not the Point

Sunday school was on "Give and Go."

This Sunday is our church's missions commitment Sunday. It's the one time of the year that we take our Faith Promise Missions Commitments and tally up our total for 2013. This Commitment includes several aspects: faith, a promise, and the whole idea of missions.

Faith doesn't mean that you save up enough money for the year, check your savings account and say, "Yep. I can do ___ every week." Faith is stepping out without knowing how God will provide and making a Promise or a commitment to come through week after week with the money.

Lest you think, "Man, this church is all about money!" let me tell you this: I know we're not going to be the biggest giving class in the church! ☺ You're poor. I've mentioned over and over that giving is about sacrifice and faithfulness. Are you sacrificing? Maybe $.50 per week is a sacrifice for you. Maybe more, maybe less... have you committed it?

Let me be clear... the Faith Promise Missions is a commitment that is above your tithe (which is 10% of all money you get), and Faith Promise is separate from your weekly Home Missions

Church Planters offering that we just took to Heartland last week. Our Pastor has cast the vision for our church to be involved in the Church Planters Conference, and every year our church's Christmas offering goes toward that conference. What we are doing with the TOF Home Missions offering every week is just adding (as we give week by week) to the whole church's offering.

Perhaps we should have stated our summaries more clearly, but we do not want to think too highly of ourselves. Giving is selfless not selfish, and we are giving under the whole church, of course, but contributing weekly in class instead of at one time in the Christmas offering only.

Praise God for the contribution our class was able to make! For what it's worth, I commend you for your part in giving sacrificially and faithfully.

"Did You Bring Your Dollar?" Part 1

This was a $1/week offering we emphasized. Part 1...

When we first introduced you to our Home Missions Offering, we said that pretty much all we're looking for is $1 from each of you. Remember the little catch phrase you asked each other: "Did you bring your dollar?"

I want to revive that.

We only have a few months (like, 12 Sundays!) before we leave for the Heartland trip, and we want to take a bundle of money from our youth group to give away to the church planters. But... that means we have to have a bundle of money.

Giving is spiritual. It's not about the money... it's about your walk with God. If you're not giving, you're not obedient to Scripture. That's why we encourage you to give. It's a spiritual discipline, just like reading your Bible, praying, guarding your mouth and thoughts...

Giving doesn't have to be about the amount. It's about faithfulness and sacrifice. Have you been faithfully giving recently? If not, how about bringing a dollar to our offering each week? How about making up for the past weeks you've missed?

Sacrifice is giving up a part of yourself. If $.50 every week is a sacrifice to you, great! If $1 is no sacrifice to you and you could easily give a dollar a week, what would it take for you to have to give by faith? "God, where's this $5 going to come from this week?" "God, where's this $_____ going to come from this week?" If the commitment is from God and for God, He will make sure that you are taken care of. But what does sacrifice look like to you? Fill in the blank above. Then bring that amount every week. All through Jr. High and High School (even before I had a job), I always tried to commit more and more each year, so that by the time I was a sophomore, God was able to provide $5/week for missions, and up to $10/week by the time I graduated. It was a sacrifice, but God always provided.

Faithfulness is about keeping to what you know you should be doing. It takes discipline. It takes... remembering. "I forgot." That's just an excuse, not a reason. Faithfulness is... always. Always being there when needed, always giving, always keeping up... Are you being faithful? I think the fact that our offerings have slipped a little (like, $4/week for the past few months) is an indication 1) that I haven't been mentioning it much, and 2) that we could use a reminder to be faithful.

So, what we're going to do is have an offering time on Sundays AND one Wednesdays. We will still shoot for $1/week from each of you, but it will be in front of you TWICE a week now to help you remember. Go ahead and ask each other every Sunday and Wednesday... "Did you bring your dollar?"

"Did You Bring Your Dollar?" Part 2

This was a $1/week offering we emphasized. Part 2...

Giving is being a faithful steward of what God has given you.

You've been given a gift that is way bigger than you, and, as a Christian, you're expected to use it in a way that benefits others.

That's what stewards did in the Bible days. That is what you should do as a Christian.

One way you've been blessed is by being saved. You were given God's Son when you got saved, and your job is to spread the gospel (good news) to the lost. In addition, as a Christian, your "job" is much bigger than that. Since you're serving GOD in everything you do, it doesn't matter what other people think, because they're not going to be the ones judging you. God will. So please God.

You please God in being obedient to His Word. Giving is one aspect of obedience, and God expects sacrifice and faithfulness, like the note said last week.

"Did you bring your dollar?" We're saying that now on Sundays and Wednesdays. Say it to each other. "Did you bring your dollar?"

Is that legalism? No. Legalism means that people add rules in order to be saved. This isn't about being saved or lost. This is about being a faithful steward of what God has given you.

Has God blessed you? God's blessed me! I want to sacrifice and faithfully give so that others can have those same blessings on their lives too! I love God and I love other people, and I want them to experience the same amazing blessings on their lives that I've experienced.

That's what giving is all about. It's not about the money. Money's easy to get. God owns everything. He created it. What's He need money for?! He doesn't. Giving is much deeper than just... money. Giving is about spiritual things. "Did you bring your dollar?"

"Did You Bring Your Dollar?" Part 3

This was a $1/week offering we emphasized. Part 3...

Everyone forgot on Wednesday. Everyone except Bro. Ken, that is. He was seeding people with $1s for the offering... on certain conditions. They had to run around the room yelling "I LOVE

TEXAS!" That's child abuse, Bro. Ken!

Well, today we're taking our offering again. We are taking it on Sundays and Wednesdays now to help us remember.

Giving is not about the money. Giving is about spiritual growth. Do you desire to be an obedient Christian? Are you trying to grow in the Lord? Giving will be a part of any stable Christian's life.

This is the third note in a row with the same title: "Did you bring your dollar?"

So... did you? If not, see Bro. Ken. Maybe he'll make you do something ridiculous again.

If you forgot today, there's always Wednesday.

"Did You Bring Your Dollar?" Part 4

This was a $1/week offering we emphasized. Part 4...

Okay. Here we go again. Did you bring your dollar?

You might be thinking, "Wait a minute... what's this dollar for again?!"

This January we are taking a bunch of people to Heartland for the Church Planting Conference. Every year around Christmas, our church takes an offering to give to the church planters, and the Teens of Faith always tries to donate, as well. That's what this offering is all about.

It's not about the money. It's not a replacement for your tithe or missions. It's all about sacrificing and being faithful.

Faithful means remembering. Did you remember tonight? No?

Well then what are you willing to do for a dollar? Maybe Bro. Ken will give you some money to do something ridiculous again. PLEASE don't make us say that we love the Cowboys, Bro. Ken! That's worse than Texas!

Great Offerings Are a Reflection Of Spiritual Things

Offerings are not about the money... they're about your being obedient to Scripture.

Giving is about your spiritual walk with God. A Christian who loves God can't help but give sacrificially and faithfully.

We've already been able to see God bless over the past few weeks of our increased attention to the offerings. I don't think it's because we're taking 2 offerings per week, either. I think it's because you're starting to see that giving is a spiritual discipline that you should be learning now, while you don't have a ton to give.

"Did you bring your dollar?" That question can be just as appropriate to ask each other as "What did you read in your Bible this week?" They're both spiritual questions. They both help you grow spiritually.

Does that make sense? I love talking to you about money, because I can sincerely mean it when I say that it's not about the money. It's not! It's about your spiritual growth.

If you're growing in the Lord, giving will be a part of it. So, praise God that He's blessing your sacrifice and faithfulness over the past couple weeks. We've been able to add one more church planter to the board, as you can see. That represents a lot of giving over the past couple weeks!

Keep up the good work.

Two Words To Sum Up Non-Missionaries (Or One Word, Perhaps)

This note was during our missions emphasis month...

Praise the Lord for your prayers and giving. Missions can be summarized in those two words: *pray* and *give* (that is, if you're not going). Perhaps a better all-in-one word might be this: surrender.

Missions is not about giving. It's not about money. It's not about financial support. It's not about missionaries coming through and asking for handouts.

Missions is about surrendering to the Lord. Missions is about someone who has said, "My life is a living sacrifice. I am letting God have my life to do whatever He wills with it." Whether that is giving or going is up to God, but ALL of us should at the very least be surrendered.

Have you surrendered? Are you surrendered?

Surrendered people give. Giving is an outflow of surrender. Giving is NOT a requirement... it's a response.

Surrendered people pray. Are you faithful to pray for missions?

First, surrender. Once you do that, the rest just falls into place.

The Order Of Our Giving

This note came after a church planting conference we attended...

We've been saving up all year to be able to give to the needs of church planters! That's what giving is all about.

Giving is not about "...and it shall be given unto you."

It's about the first part: "Give..."

Do you give? Do you give by faith? Do you give faithfully? Do you give cheerfully?

All last year you did, and those who went to the conference were able to see the blessings of your giving. Giving is not about the money. It's not about God's blessing YOU for giving.

Giving is simply about obedience to Scripture.

Today marks a couple checkpoints in giving. First, we are re-starting our Home Missions fund back at zero. We gave it all away, and now we are starting over.

Second, today is Missions Commitment Sunday in church. The order goes like this:

1. Tithe
2. Faith Promise missions (today's commitment)
3. Home Missions $1 weekly offering.

Do #1 and #2 first.

Then, after you give, trust God to be faithful to His promise and return His blessings. That's not WHY we give… but it's a cool bonus!

Here Are a Few Ideas To Help You Give Your $1 Per Week

How are you doing on giving? Are you working toward earning money each week?

"Mom, I need to have a dollar by Sunday or Bro. Ryan will grill me again. I know I can scrounge up the money if I try, but are there some chores I can do a little extra each week to get a dollar?"

Or… "Dad, how much can I spend at Jack-in-the-Box? $5? Okay, if I only spend $3.50, can you give me to difference to bring for my offering this Sunday?"

Or… "Mom, when you're at Costco can you get me a box of those king-sized MM's so I can go door-to-door and sell them for camp? I promise I'll pay you back with my earnings, and I'll tithe on the profits, I'll give some to missions, and I want to get another dollar from each box for the Teens of Faith Home Missions Fund."

There are LOTS of ways to get a dollar every week, and it's probably only because you didn't think about trying (laziness) if you can't get it by Sunday. Do you think $1 is fair? I'd say God would think it is, and giving is a spiritual thing, anyway. If you don't learn to give, it's not a problem with your budget as much as it's a problem with your heart. I'm telling you (from God), if you learn to give, He'll bless it. He promises to, so try Him and see! It's a very cool cycle to be in on.

Giving Away $8k Is Good For Us and For Them

This was anticipating the church planters conference...

This week, several people from our church will be heading to Heartland for the Church Planters Conference. It is a good chance to see the college as well as a way for our church to be a blessing to several church planters. Like Pastor announced a couple weeks ago, we raised over $8,000 through our Christmas offering! What a blessing to give.

Giving is a blessing TO US... not only to the recipient. The fact that we are able to give is a testimony of God's financial goodness to us. We want to accept God's gifts with the mindset that HE is the owner, and WE are the stewards. We are just using His money the way He wants us to.

Are you a giver? A couple weeks ago in our 1 Corinthians series we talked about giving. Paul just lays it out there like it's what every Christian should do. Maybe he did that because giving is what every Christian should do.

Did you get your giving contribution statement back from the church for last year? Did you give? Did you stretch your faith through giving? Did you see God provide and bless? Did you put God to the test?

Hopefully your answer to all those questions is "yes." Giving is YOUR benefit. The only person missing out by not giving is you. Think about it... it's a win-win!

Today is More Talk About Something You

Don't Have

Brains?

Coolness?

Good looks?

Well, you might not have any of those things, but that's not what we're talking about today. Today's sermon is a continuation of last week's talk about money.

Money is something you probably don't have much of. Right? If you're rich, you don't flaunt it, at least. That's good.

Most young people have pretty much $.27 to their name. When they spend a quarter on that gum ball they dreamed of, that leaves them with exactly $.02. Two pennies. Like the two mites that the widow had.

Not much.

But if you can learn to use the LITTLE you have right now, God will bless you with MUCH later (Luke 16:10).

Wise choices should show up in every area of life. When you ask, "What is the wise thing to do?" (our series in Proverbs), you are affecting your WHOLE life. This series isn't JUST about your spiritual life, although that's the main part. It is about your... life!

School life. Homework life. Job life. Money life. Friends life. Etc.

Let God affect your life. He'll make every part of it better.

Miracles That YOU Helped With

This was a $1/week offering we emphasized...

Over the course of last year through the Sunday morning offerings, our class raise about $250 for the church planters. Last week at the Church Planters Conference at Heartland in Oklahoma City, I was able to give it all away. It went fast!

I looked at my envelope on Wednesday morning and counted the $20 bills that we got from the ATM. One, two, three, four, five. *That's all that's left?!* I got so excited about giving to every guy I could... I ran out of money!

Truly, miracles still happen. A bunch of poor Baptists got together and gave away over $400,000 in three days! Plus, they committed a combined $10,000 per month to various church plants all over America. It was incredible.

And you had a part in it.

Seriously! Even though most of you were not able to go to the conference this year (except for Alisha, Sarah and Michael C.), you were still able to have a part in it by giving. Isn't that what Bro. Tomlinson emphasized last week? That—practically speaking—the bulk of Christians will not be called to go, but only to give.

If you ever gave any amount—even if it was only $1—you had a part in the Church Planting Conference. You were one small sliver of the miracle that God performed.

The best part about God's work is that no one knows who the givers were. GOD gets all the glory. Nobody marked their dollar bill when they put it in the offering and said, "Whoever this goes to, I want them to know that *I* put it in the offering!" Nope.

When God gets the credit, life is so much better. Thank you for your involvement. I love you all, and I was proud to represent you at the conference last week. I wish you could have been there. Maybe next year...

Congratulations!

YOU FINISHED! Now keep going...

The Christian journey is **more of a path than a destination**.

Now that you have finished this devotional, do not stop your journey. **Keep going.** This path is good.

Visit **RyanRench.com** and sign up for email updates. I am always working on *something,* and my email list gets first dibs on upcoming books.

If you want to keep going, this is a good place to start. Not only will you find other helpful articles, but you can look up other books, too. I try to make sure everything I write is helpful to you, so go check it out.

I look forward to hearing from you!

Author's Note

I'm a youth pastor at a church in California. The BEST part about my job is when my teens "get it." Know what I mean?

I mean when teens learn to love God—like, REALLY love Him where it's not pretend—that's when life is amazing.

You want to make your pastor and youth pastor proud? Yes? Then here's my advice: GET IT.

Once you "get it" about your walk with God, it's no longer a drudgery. Once God is REAL to you, walking with Him is fun! Sinning makes you feel like you hurt your friend, so repentance is more natural.

I LOVE it when I have those teens that "get it." Not for MY sake, but for THEIRS.

Be that.

Once you "get it," it makes everything better—your God is pleased, your parents are pleased, your pastor is happy... even your sister might enjoy life around you!

I sure love you. Even without knowing you, I want God's best for you.

Love God. Love others. Do right.

About the

Author

Author's Words: I repeatedly demand that my teens call me *The Pope of Temecula*. They smirk and pat my bald spot with a condescending "There, there, Brother Ryan..." I'm the bigger man. I don't get mad. I'll accept *youth pastor* as my title instead.

Stuffy Bio: Ryan Rench serves as the youth director and associate pastor of Calvary Baptist Church in Temecula, CA, under his father's leadership, Pastor W. M. Rench. Ryan's family moved to Temecula in 1986 to plant the church where Ryan was reared and is now on staff. He earned his Bachelor's and Master's Degree in ministry from Heartland Baptist Bible College and Graduate School in 2008 and 2010.

Ryan Rench married his wife, Jamie, in 2008. They have one son named Abe (July 2012) and two daughters: Charlotte (March 2014) and Gwen (February 2016).

Ryan blogs at <u>RyanRench.com</u> and has published several books, including *BIBS: Big Idea Bible Study* and *A Case For Bible College*, available from **Calvary Baptist Publications** (<u>CalvaryBaptist.pub</u>.)

Let's Connect!
One cool thing about no-name authors (me) is that they are readily accessible. If you contact me, I'll respond. In fact, I'll

probably be giddy. Usually it's only my wife and mom who read my stuff, and even THAT is hit and miss (I force them to proof my books just so I know they've read them). **Here's where I live:**

- **Email**: RyanRench@gmail.com (this is the TOP contact)
- **The Twitters**: @RyanARench (the Twitters is my fav!)
- **FaceBooks**: /RyanRenchcom (I sort of know how to work the FaceBooks. Sort of.)
- **Website**: RyanRench.com (my other contact info is here)

Books By the

Author

THE CHRISTIAN TEEN DEVOTIONAL
This is a collection of almost 200 notes from 7 years as a youth pastor.

* * *

MY DEVOTIONAL JOURNAL

This 7x10" journal includes all the devotional entries from *The Christian Teen Devotional* as well as blank lines and journal prompt questions to fill out.

* * *

BIBS: BIG IDEA BIBLE STUDY

This book teaches you how to read and understand your Bible using observation, interpretation and application. It is the perfect starting point for knowing how to hear from God through His Word.

* * *

BIBS DEVOTIONALS

This daily and weekly devotional uses the BIBS process to go both deep and wide in Scripture. Each day includes a broad reading assignment and a simple writing task. Get both volumes:

ONE YEAR (Blue): Covers several books of the Bible over the course of one year.

PROVERBS (Red): Covers the book of Proverbs over the course of 30 weeks.

* * *

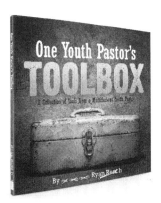

ONE YOUTH PASTOR'S TOOLBOX

This book is one youth pastor's proven collection of book reviews, game ideas, activity notes, sermon series and more.

* * *

A CASE FOR BIBLE COLLEGE

Are you considering Bible college? This book covers:

1) Why we encourage high school graduates to attend a year of Bible college, and

2) How to prepare for Bible college once you have committed.

* * *

A CASE FOR BEING TIMELESS

This book was a series of minibooks that we used for our Preaching Rally. It explains what being timeless is and how it might look in our churches.

* * *

THE PREACHING RALLY

This book is an in-depth review of how we plan and run our content-driven one-day youth conference: The Preaching Rally. It's more than a youth rally. This book explains how.

* * *

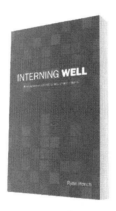

INTERNING WELL

If you plan on interning at a church, this book is full of real-life training lessons that our interns have learned over the years. This book is required reading for our interns.

* * *

"A CASE FOR" MINIBOOK SERIES

Dating God's Way. Several tips on following God's leading in dating.
Sunday Evening Church. Why our church loves our evening services.
Reverence. Why reverence is not a bad thing—when done right.
Saturday Soul-Winning. Some benefits of regular Saturday outreach.
Why We Have Church. A doctrinal and practical look at the
institution of the church.

64198030R00141

Made in the USA
Lexington, KY
01 June 2017